GRIT, GRACE & GRAVITAS

The Three Keys to Transforming Leadership, Presence, and Impact

RESOURCE GUIDE & WORKBOOK

**BY JANE FIRTH, MSOD
AND ANDREA ZINTZ, Ph.D.**

Grit, Grace, & Gravitas
Resource Guide & Workbook
The Three Keys to Transforming Leadership, Presence, and Impact

Copyright © 2023 by
Jane Firth, MSOD, and Andrea Zintz, Ph.D.

ISBN: 979-8-9871697-0-4

Cover design: Caroline Chen
Interior design: FormattedBooks

This workbook is dedicated to you and the extraordinary potential you possess to elevate your leadership, your presence, and your impact. It was designed to help you integrate the social emotional skills that distinguish exemplary leaders and serve to accelerate the achievement of your personal and professional aspirations. It will help you understand how to evolve your talents and abilities and increase your competence as a leader. It will help you develop the depth and contribution of your presence. It will help you shape your impact and the legacy you are building in critically important ways.

CONTENTS

PREFACE

In our extensive work with clients over the years, we've had the privilege of listening deeply to what is in the hearts and minds of the people we coach and advise. Our work with leaders in their various industries and work environments, along with our research, has led us to identify critical qualities and behaviors that form the foundation and character of truly exemplary leaders. We've found that while every leader is unique, exemplary leaders possess and lead through a combination of three critical factors. The character and heart of their leadership are composed of the following: 1) they have *grit*—an uncompromising commitment to performance excellence and strategic focus, and 2) they have *gravitas*—a depth of professional knowledge and competence that contribute to excellence in performance, and most importantly, 3) they have *grace*—they relate to others constructively in considerate, empathetic, and genuinely caring ways.

Integrating the skills and qualities of *grace* into our approaches, behaviors, connection with people, and our demeanor transforms imbalances in our *grit* and *gravitas* that have been getting in the way and causing problems.

We've created this resource guide and workbook at the request of leaders who have read our book, *Grit, Grace, & Gravitas*. They've asked for a practical guide to help them accelerate their evolution as leaders and put the skills and qualities of exemplary leadership into action for themselves. We've included, chapter by chapter, room for you to reflect and shape the practical applications of *grit, grace,* and *gravitas* that are important to you.

You can use this workbook to:

- Create a more compelling and impactful presence, evolve as a leader, and be a contribution in ways that will be important and meaningful to you.

- Increase your ability to bring out the best in yourself and those you lead.

- Increase your skills in dealing with the emotional realities and performance challenges of leadership that otherwise get in the way of solutions, innovation, and progress.

Chapter 1

INTRODUCTION TO THE WORKBOOK

As you use this workbook and clarify what *grit, grace,* and *gravitas* mean to *you* as a person and as a leader, you will see how to elevate the contribution and impact of your presence. You will have the opportunity to connect in meaningful ways with your highest aspirations. You will be able to clarify the steps and practical actions you want to take to evolve the nature and substance of your leadership.

Let's begin with a short review of *grit, grace,* and *gravitas,* what they are, and why it is important to consider them together. What has come to light over decades of work with leaders is that while every leader is unique, exemplary leaders have integrated values, qualities, a nd skills that relate to the following:

- Their *grit* reflects an uncompromising commitment to performance excellence and strategic focus. *Grit* is about perseverance, intentionality, purpose, and a powerful drive for getting past obstacles and resistance.

- Their *gravitas* reflects a depth of their professional knowledge, experience, and competence that contributes to excellence in their performance. *Gravitas* speaks to a depth of knowledge and experience, wisdom gained, competence, and confidence based on experience.

But, most importantly:

Exemplary leaders have *grace*—the game changer in the way *grace* transforms the impact of their *grit* and *gravitas*. The constructive power of *grace* increases a leader's effectiveness with people; it elevates their ability to bring out the best in themselves and others, increases their value to the organization, and enhances their ability to help their teams innovate and collaborate. Leaders with *grace* relate to others constructively. They are developed in two critically important ways.

The first is that they have developed their *reaction management* skills. As a result, they've become more self-aware, they are skillful in managing their own emotional reactions, and they have developed the skills to be able to elevate the emotional operating state of others; they can lift morale and engage their teams with meaning, vision, and purpose.

The second is they have developed a high degree of *relationship intelligence* skills. They have an elevated capacity to relate to others constructively in considerate, respectful, empathetic, appreciative, and genuinely caring ways.

Grace rests on two pillars

Grace rests on two pillars of reaction management and relationship intelligence. The skills and qualities contained in these two pillars are the source of our constructive power.

Consider how leaders can lean into their constructive power when they have to deal with difficult people and situations. They are developing themselves to take constructive approaches and their behavior is constructive, as is the quality of how they connect with people and their way of being—their demeanor. Exemplary leaders work to model this consistently through their efforts with individuals, their groups, their divisions, and throughout their organization as a whole. They work to bring people together in meaningful ways; they can bring people into alignment to accomplish the goals that matter. All these factors shape a leader's presence and impact. It also shapes the culture, which we will talk about further on.

Grit, grace, and *gravitas* have an unusual, profound relationship. *Grit* and *gravitas* represent essential leadership qualities and skills. But when a leader's *grit* is missing elements of *grace,* it can be experienced by others as harsh, rigid, inflexible, and closed-minded. Lacking in *grace,* others may interpret a leader's *grit* as offensive, inconsiderate, overbearing, or unappreciative. Consequently, people can be left feeling unsupported, resentful, less motivated, and less engaged.

Recall one or two leaders you've found difficult to work with. Make a note for yourself about an experience or situation that comes to mind. What imbalances in their *grit* and/or *gravitas* can you identify?

_____

_____

_____

_____

_____

_____

_____

_____

Lacking in *grace,* a leader's *grit* can be perceived as harsh, demanding, and domineering. Lacking in *grace,* a leader's *gravitas* can be perceived as arrogant, condescending, and disrespectful. *Grace* provides the defining difference—it's the game changer—it modulates and balances a leader's *grit* and *gravitas* with constructive power.

What are some initial thoughts, given the example that came to mind, about how *grace* can change or improve a leader's impact when their *grit* and *gravitas* are out of balance?

_____

_____

_____

_____

_____

_____

_____

_____

There will be opportunities throughout this workbook to consider how imbalances can get in the way, and how to use the constructive power of *grace* to evolve as a leader.

Here's an example. Let's consider what changed in the imbalance of Craig's *gravitas*. (Craig's full story is on pages 15-20 in our book.) His arrogance, which reflected his need for self-importance, was replaced by an increased awareness and regard for the importance of what others can contribute. He gained humility and a willingness to listen to others. He accomplished this by facing the negative impact he was having, choosing to take the feedback he was given, and doing the work of building new habits. Craig was able to listen to feedback that was divergent from his self-perceptions and make a choice to see how he could build new habits to be a better leader. He wound up improving his reputation and turning the negative impact he was having into one that was positive and empowering.

Craig's willingness to face his foibles and flaws allowed him to form new habits. He succeeded in elevating the substance and quality of his leadership, his presence, and his impact.

Remember, constructive power is always within your reach. Using the skills and tools provided in this section of the workbook, your access to your constructive power will strengthen and increase.

Chapter 2

DEFINING EXECUTIVE PRESENCE

It's important to remember that you have a very distinct, unique presence, as unique as your fingerprints—and the impact of your presence is felt hundreds of times a day by those you live, lead, and work with.

If you want to understand how to elevate your presence and improve the quality of the impact you are having on the people you lead, you can gather feedback to learn how others currently perceive your approaches, behaviors, the quality of your connection with them, and your demeanor. This information can reveal blind spots, ineffective habits, foibles, and flaws that you may not realize are getting in the way of achieving your higher aspirations as a leader. Even though you may not like hearing some of the feedback, if you provide yourself with an objective lens, you can use what you learn to elevate your growth and development.

Take a moment now to consider your impact: What kind of impact do you want to have? For example: Do you want your impact to be inclusive, warm, and welcoming? Do you want to impact others in ways that open things up for important dialogues to take place? Start to identify the qualities you want your impact to provide. Make some notes for yourself.

Here's a starting place:

What are a few initial thoughts about how you see the impact you are currently having?

_____

_____

_____

_____

_____

A simple formula for elevating your presence...

Consider the following to understand the means through which you impact people through your presence:

The formula is this: A+B+C+D = IoP:

Approaches, **Behaviors**, the quality of **Connection** with others, and one's overall **Demeanor** are what generate the Impact of one's Presence.

What further thoughts are coming to your mind about how your presence may be impacting those you lead and work with? Is there something about how you are impacting those you lead and work with that you would like to change for the better? Let's look at this in terms of the formula above:

_____

_____

_____

_____

_____

Your approaches convey your attitude, frame of mind, and how you feel about what it is you are addressing. This can include the position you take in facing and addressing people and situations. Are your approaches generally constructive? Do you give any thought to how you are going to approach someone or something, such as asking yourself a question like: What is the best way to approach this?

What are some thoughts about the **approaches** you find yourself taking? Is there something about the approaches you find yourself taking that you would like to change for the better?

_____

_____

_____

_____

_____

_____

_____

_____

What do your **behaviors** reflect? What intentions and values are reflected in your actions? Are there aspects of your behavior you would like to change for the better?

_____

_____

_____

_____

_____

_____

_____

_____

The quality of your **connection** with people helps you convey how you want the people around you to feel. What thoughts are coming to your mind about the quality of how you connect with people? What is it you would like people to feel? For example: *I want people to feel my appreciation,* or *I want people to come away from interactions we have with a sense that they are valued and respected.* What would you like to improve about the quality of your connection with people?

_____

_____

_____

_____

_____

_____

Your **demeanor** reflects and broadcasts your state of mind and attitude. Your attitudes are visible in your facial expressions, your voice, your body language, whether you are attentive or distracted, agitated, or relaxed, ruffled or ready, irritated, impatient, or calm and collected.

Are you aware of how your **demeanor** impacts others? Generally, how would you describe your demeanor? What does your demeanor reflect? For instance, does my demeanor consistently reflect some combination of inclusiveness, supportiveness, and encouragement? Remember, there are no wrong answers. What would you like to improve in your demeanor?

_____

_____

_____

_____

_____

_____

What kind of impact do you want your **demeanor** to have?

_____

_____

_____

_____

_____

_____

_____

In the space below list some initial steps you can take to improve your approaches, behaviors, the quality of how you connect with people, and your demeanor:

_____

_____

_____

_____

_____

_____

_____

How can we improve? Let's look at how imbalances in _grit_ and _gravitas_ get in the way and some of the ways we can elevate the impact of our approaches, behaviors, the quality of our connection with others, and our demeanor...

Imbalances in our _grit_ and our _gravitas_ are reflected in our ABCD. Here are some of the imbalances that get in the way of intentions and aspirations, causing problems.

To help you understand imbalances that might be getting in the way, you can use the descriptions of imbalances provided below. Before you do, remember the purpose is for growth and development, NOT for criticizing and finding fault with yourself and others. The examples we cite are meant to jog your thought process. Not every listed descriptive example will apply.

Let's begin by considering the imbalances that can show up in a leader's *grit* as in too much *grit*, or too little *grit*:

Too much *grit* can look like:

- ***Close-minded, dug in:*** With too much *grit*, someone can be inflexible, rigid, dug in, stubborn, and exhibit an inability to consider the merits of other perspectives. Someone who comes across in this way tends to lack an inclination for cooperation and to value others for their input and information, especially if they don't agree with their thinking. They may also tend to operate from an investment in their assumptions without verifying their validity.

- ***Dominating, controlling, my way or the highway:*** Behaving in a domineering, demanding, insistent, or inconsiderate manner; others experience this kind of person as controlling. This aspect in someone often has a commanding influence on others, at times using ultimatums, making their dissatisfaction apparent, and indicating others will either conform to his or her desires or else be excluded. Others can experience this element in someone's *grit* as dismissive, demeaning, and disrespectful.

- ***Micromanaging, not empowering others:*** Someone who micromanages others exercises excessive control and involvement in the details. Rather than empower others, this type of imbalance causes someone to be inclined to criticize and find fault, breathe down people's necks or "do it myself to get it done right." A couple of consequences of this imbalance in someone's *grit* are the lost benefits that talent development makes possible, and how people are compromised when a leader withholds critical information and opportunities to advance.

- ***Blaming and judgmental:*** Someone with this tendency is often dominated by their internal negative criticizer that is judging and criticizing themselves and others in disempowering ways. They abdicate their power and responsibility to address matters at hand in a constructive way. They use judgments and criticism to find fault, be right, and justify in place of a desire to restore a more open, objective, and collaborative connection; they are often impatient and irritated.

- ***Oppositional, confrontational, and combative:*** Someone with these imbalances in their *grit* takes an interpersonal approach that is openly competitive and focused on winning at all costs. Sometimes they use below-the-belt tactics to diminish or discredit others to achieve an advantage. These behaviors can be experienced as aggressive and disruptive, resulting in short- and/or long-term consequences. They obstruct progress, create disunity, and leave ill will, distrust, and resentment in their wake.

Too little *grit* can look like:

- ***Ambivalent and conflicted, lacking the ability to select priorities and be decisive:*** Someone with this imbalance in their *grit* has trouble making decisions in a timely way. Their fear of making a wrong decision leaves them confused and ambivalent. The fear of failing causes overthinking and over-analyzing and gets in the way of choosing priorities and making strategic decisions.

- *Lack of clarity when giving or receiving directions and setting expectations:* Someone with this imbalance in their *grit,* on the one hand, doesn't set clear priorities or ensure that others have the information they need to execute plans and next steps. On the other hand, when receiving directions and the expectations involved, they don't always clarify because they don't want to feel or look stupid or be perceived as annoying by asking questions.

- *Discomfort with power, one's own and others':* When someone has this imbalance in their *grit,* they feel uncomfortable with their own power and with the power others have. They may feel intimidated or lack confidence. Reluctant to stand up for themselves, they may be too eager to please and not want to make waves. Not wanting to impose on others, they bend over backwards; they take on too little or too much in tasks or projects, they don't push back in moments that matter, and they don't set boundaries. This leaves them feeling overwhelmed and burdened, which can lead to burnout.

- *Difficulty holding others accountable:* Someone with this imbalance in their *grit* avoids the discomfort of confronting someone who isn't meeting their responsibilities, expectations, or coming through as agreed. They may avoid having difficult conversations because they don't want to seem demanding; they may confuse the importance of holding people accountable with being seen as overbearing. They often have a fear of conflict and an aversion to contentious dialogue with people who have difficulty being held accountable. Examples include people who act like the victim, people who become defensive and righteous and always have reasons for why things are the way they are, and mercurial people who refuse to be pinned down to what is, in fact, their responsibility.

- ***Avoiding difficult conversations and emotionally charged situations:*** Someone with this imbalance in their *grit lacks* skills for understanding emotions, reactions, and how to approach them constructively. Without these skills, one lacks the ability and confidence to access their emotions. Situations such as these trigger a threat rather than an opportunity. Without relationship intelligence skills, suppressed feelings can generate reactions expressed in unconstructive ways. The consequence often leads to misunderstandings and blocked progress.

- ***Inconsistent behavior with a consequential effect of seeming or actually being unreliable:*** Someone with this imbalance in their *grit* lacks focus—they often lose the thread of where they are headed. They may have a pattern of showing up late for appointments and meetings, not holding up their end, and not following through or keeping their word, which causes doubts as to their dependability and trustworthiness. They often find justifications for their behavior such as "being too busy." They can sound cavalier, as if they lack concern and regard for others.

- ***Disorganized and lacking structures:*** Someone with this imbalance in their *grit* resists using structured, systematic, or agreed upon approaches. Their imbalance can result in becoming disorganized and overwhelmed. They may keep everything they have to do in their head or have a disregard for protocols. They resist using systems, for example, on their computer or journal to help them prioritize, complete tasks, and reach deadlines. Often their office can be messy and disorganized with files piled high on every surface. People with this imbalance in their *grit* have a pattern of creating chaos and causing confusion for themselves and others. They create obstacles that increase the difficulty in getting work done.

Here are some examples to consider regarding imbalances of too much *gravitas*:

- *Hubris, expressing opinions with an air of superiority:* Because of their considerable experience and expertise, someone with this imbalance in their *gravitas* often dominates conversations in what feels like a condescending manner. Without realizing it, they speak with a careless lack of humility. Their arrogance causes them to correct and criticize others and come across with an air of superiority. Collaborating, cooperating, or functioning as a constructive member of a team can seem unimportant to them in situations where they believe they have superior knowledge and experience.

- *Thinking one's opinion is the only one that matters:* Someone with this imbalance in their *gravitas* often goes on and on, seeming pedantic, speaking only on "send," and not listening to "receive." Someone with this tendency talks over others and interrupts; they can exhibit an automatic pattern of selective listening. They seem to ignore, minimize, or invalidate the importance of what others have to say. These tendencies prevent them from recognizing the value inherent in listening to others. As a consequence, the valuable perspectives, ideas, and opinions others could otherwise contribute are lost. Another consequence is that people can be left frustrated, potentially resentful, and disengaged.

- *Needing to be the center of attention, stealing, or hogging the spotlight:* Someone with this imbalance in their *gravitas* is overly concerned with their own desires, needs, or interests. They make sure they are the center of attention. They may take the credit for work that others have contributed or originated.

- ***Acting in an obstructive and controlling manner:*** Someone with this imbalance in their *gravitas* makes it more challenging to accomplish what needs to be done. Their controlling behavior interferes with and obstructs the flow of progress, using justifications such as "I'm just being a devil's advocate." They delay progress and decision making in unconstructive ways.

- ***Gravitas others perceive as unapproachable and intimidating:*** While it's not the person or expert's intent, sometimes someone with *gravitas* in their field or profession can be regarded as intimidating and unapproachable because of their considerable knowledge when, in fact, they may be shy and introverted. Someone with this imbalance in their *gravitas* may lack the skills that would allow them to be more connected and at ease in collaborating with their teammates and colleagues. Unlike someone who lauds their knowledge over people, these are people who, because of their shyness and introversion, wind up isolated and excluded. One unintended consequence of their not being seen as approachable is the loss of the valuable contributions their considerable knowledge could bring to light.

- ***Inflating one's gravitas competitively at the expense of creating synergy with others:*** Using one's *gravitas* to assert and protect one's status as a source of value, either because one's contribution has been misappropriated by a member of one's team or someone is directly or indirectly diminishing what one brings to the table. Someone with this imbalance in their *gravitas* defaults to establishing some form of protective boundary in the former, or resorts to competitive power plays in the latter. Both result in a loss of productive connection, collaboration, and engagement.

Too little *gravitas* can look like:

- **Unclaimed *gravitas*, coming across to others as a lack in strength, stature, and significance:** Unlike humility, which downplays *recognized* abilities, unclaimed *gravitas* reflects an inability or a reticence to adequately recognize one's depth of knowledge and experience. Someone with this imbalance in their *gravitas* robs themselves of the quiet confidence, credibility, and stature that comes from authentically recognizing their *gravitas*. Some of the repercussions can take the form of being discounted, passed over, disregarded, or excluded.

- **An absence of internal permission to own one's power and influence:** Someone with this imbalance in their *gravitas* has a lack of confidence in their knowledge and experience, which also results in an imbalance in their *grit*—the reluctance to push back, take a stand, or contribute an idea, a perspective, or an observation that could be of value to the matters at hand. The imbalance of one's *gravitas* reflects an absence of internal permission to express one's power and influence. It is all too easy for someone with this imbalance to minimize their accomplishments, their growth, and their development. Their self-confidence suffers as a result. Retreating from important and meaningful opportunities, their lack of confidence impedes or blocks their progress and gets in the way of achieving their considerable potential. As a result, they take on too little; they play too small.

- **Overcompensating, trying too hard to be seen as credible:** Someone with this imbalance in their *gravitas* often tries to prove their value and worthiness. In their efforts to be perceived as capable and credible, they often take on more than they can handle. They also try too hard to be liked and accepted. Someone with this imbalance in their *gravitas* may accept responsibilities without understanding how to build the appropriate platforms and garner the necessary advocacy, resources, and support they need to succeed. To mask their insecurities, they often present a patina of confidence; they overcompensate for a lack of authentic confidence in themselves, which has them appear inauthentic to others.

- **Lacking strategic thinking skills or lacking vision:** Someone with this imbalance in their *gravitas* loses their grasp of the big picture. Their analytic brilliance often has them get caught up in the details. Having zoomed in to analyze the details, they find themselves unable to zoom back out again to see the connections and possibilities that can lead to breakthroughs, innovation, and growth.

Reflection:

1. Take a moment to identify which imbalances of *grit* stood out for you. For each imbalance you've identified, describe the impact of this imbalance. How does this imbalance in *grit* show up in your leadership or someone else's? For instance, what impact does this imbalance have on performance, morale, and/or team dynamics?

_____

_____

_____

_____

_____

_____

_____

_____

2. Take a moment to identify which elements of *gravitas* stood out for you. For each imbalance you've identified, describe the impact of this imbalance. How does this imbalance in *gravitas* show up in your leadership or someone else's? For instance, what impact does this imbalance have on performance, morale, and/or team dynamics?

_____

_____

_____

_____

_____

_____

_____

_____

With these imbalances in mind, let's look at *grace,* which is the "home" of our constructive power, and begin to see how *grace* can serve to modify imbalances in constructive ways.

Grace unleashes constructive power to transform imbalances in a leader's presence and impact. It elevates the quality and effectiveness of a leader's interactions and influence in ways that empower people, performance, and outcomes. The skills and qualities of *grace* increase a leader's depth of knowledge and ability to transform negative human emotions and dynamics into constructive dialogue and outcomes. One of the ways it elevates a leader's impact and effectiveness is that with greater knowledge and understanding of the social-emotional skills of *grace,* leaders can bring people together through considerate, thoughtful means.

What makes this possible? Starting with the first pillar of *grace*, *reaction management*, in the following pages, let's look at some examples of reaction management skills. As a leader develops his or her ability to be aware of when they are in the *reactive zone*, their ability to press the pause button helps them regain perspective and presence of mind when an emotional reaction takes hold.

Chapter 3

THE FIRST PILLAR OF GRACE: REACTION MANAGEMENT

In this chapter, we look at the importance of reaction management, one of the two foundational pillars of *grace*. We examine how the brain deals with emotions and reactions, and how to step out of the *reactive zone* to regain our objectivity and presence of mind.

What is the reactive zone? It is a state of mind that has been triggered by something that feels threatening. Think of it like the opposite of calm. When a reaction is triggered, the amygdala part of the brain takes over, pushing us into a state such as fight or flight. While the amygdala is "in charge," our higher order thinking located in the prefrontal cortex is temporarily "disabled." The skills of reaction management enable you to move out of the amygdala's reactive state, regain your higher order objective thinking, and elevate from a reactive state to a state so you can think clearly; they also enable you to understand what triggered your reaction, the emotions and meaning of what occurred, and to decide, with calmness and clarity, how best to handle the situation at hand.

Reaction management is a pillar of strength in a leader. Why? As a leader, your reactions, and the reactions of those you lead, along with their emotional undercurrents, are of vital importance regarding the dynamics of your team and the outcomes they produce. How you handle reactions and emotions is a critical part of having an exemplary presence; how you handle reactions determines the impact you are able to have on the emotional operating states of the people you lead. It is what determines your ability to have a constructive impact that can elevate the culture of your organization.

Daily, your reactions and emotions will influence the quality of performance, the strength of engagement, and the morale of the people you lead. Through examples that follow, along with the skills discussed in this section, you'll gain a deeper understanding of how reaction management, along with the presence of mind it gives you, allows you to move beyond the initial negative states of your reactions and address breakdowns using your constructive power.

In our book there is an example of a client we call Kyle. Kyle had found himself in an uncomfortable, compromised position in an executive meeting. Following the meeting Kyle got back to his office, closed his door, and used the following process to empower his self-awareness, regain his presence of mind, and gain clarity of the steps he could take to resolve what had occurred.

In building reaction management skills, awareness is key. Think of a recent situation in which you feel or felt challenged.

Here are some questions you can ask yourself:

- What feels uncomfortable or threatening to me about this situation?

_____

_____

_____

_____

_____

_____

- What happened in this situation that doesn't "sit right" with me?

_____

_____

_____

_____

_____

- What are you experiencing in this situation? Did you notice a reaction of fight—lashing out in angry words or accusations, for example? Or a reaction of flight—wanting to get away from the person or the experience that feels threatening in some way? Do not judge yourself; just notice what occurred.

_____

_____

_____

_____

_____

- Are expectations, values, or boundaries involved? If so, what can I clarify for myself about this?

_____

_____

_____

_____

_____

_____

Emotions serve an important purpose: to help us become aware when something feels threatening. Think of emotions as part of your internal "navigation system," trying to get your attention. Many people would prefer to avoid emotions that are trying to get their attention. If our emotions weren't valuable to us, we wouldn't have them. They help us zero in on the moment that triggered our reaction. By paying attention to these signals, you can gain control in two ways: 1. You can regain your presence of mind, and 2. You can release the grip of the reaction you are having to what occurred. By pausing to ask yourself questions, you begin to take yourself out of the _reactive zone_. Your state changes from a state of reactivity to one where, as Viktor Frankl tells us, you can choose your response. You can begin to think more clearly, objectively, and strategically about how to constructively deal with the situation at hand.

It's important to tune in to the messages your emotions are sending. For example, frustration can send a message about not being able to achieve something, i.e., that you're feeling blocked in reaching a goal or not having support you were counting on. Another is anxiety, which can send a message having to do with risk, i.e., when you feel unsure about something you are trying to achieve, or you are lacking confidence in yourself and are doubting your ability.

The following are steps for moving ourselves out of the reactive zone, understanding triggers, and understanding and using the messages our emotions are sending.

Some reactions may seem harder to process and resolve. There are times when your emotions can seem to "get the better of you" so you have trouble getting out of the *reactive zone*. When the amygdala reacts to a threat taking place and higher cognitive abilities are temporarily out of reach, it is all too easy to feel a loss of control. In the more difficult reactions that occur when things don't roll off your back, there are actions you can take to get yourself out of the *reactive zone*. You can press the pause button, reflect on what happened, and identify the emotions that have been triggered. If you observe your emotions rather than judge them, you will be able to see why this emotion is trying to get your attention.

The goal is to reconnect with your ability to generate a constructive outcome. The steps we outline below help you manage reactions that are more difficult. These steps shorten the time it takes to tap into your *constructive power* and turn things around.

Think of a recent reaction you experienced. (You can use the one you worked on above or choose another.) Take each of these following steps to move yourself out of the reactive zone.

Step 1: Pause and identify.

Give yourself time to process what occurred and regain your presence of mind. This gives you space to understand your reaction and choose a constructive response.

Identify physical sensations. Are you feeling tension? Where is the discomfort? Are you gritting your teeth? Is your stomach in knots? Take a slow breath in and out in each area you've identified. As you breathe, see if you can begin to identify the emotion you are feeling.

_____

_____

_____

_____

_____

_____

Here's what happened for Kyle during the meeting with his colleagues that first triggered his reaction. He took stock of where he was feeling the tension in his body. He noticed that his hands were shaking, and he turned his attention to taking slow breaths to calm himself. He realized that he was feeling embarrassed and exposed. As he breathed into the areas of tension, he felt his hands stop shaking and felt his composure returning.

Step 2: Release the grip of your reaction and understand the emotions you are feeling.

Give yourself some privacy so you can identify the emotions you are feeling and work on what we call a *responsible release*. On a piece of paper, for your eyes only, write down the reactions you are having. What emotions are trying to get your attention? Are you feeling angry, frustrated, impatient, afraid, annoyed, resentful, excluded, or anxious? You may notice more than one emotion.

_____

_____

_____

_____

_____

_____

When Kyle took out his pad and pen, he put the word "embarrassed" at the top of the page and listed his concerns and thoughts from his experience at the meeting. He then wrote the word "anxiety" and listed his thoughts and concerns that came to his mind about his team and the risks involved with having unwisely trusted them for the information and projections needed for the meeting.

As you describe the emotions you are feeling, write down your thoughts and concerns.

_____

_____

_____

_____

_____

_____

_____

_____

_____

_____

As Kyle continued to write his feelings and thoughts, the charge lessened. And as his state changed, he regained his presence of mind. He realized that the ease with which he had been able to rely on his previous team did not transfer to this culture. He saw that the expectations in this new company required the kind of grit and rigor expected in an engineering firm. He realized that he needed to work with his team to set up rules of engagement and accountability that would serve them well.

Step 3: Gauging your progress so far.

Notice if your reactions are lessening, remaining the same, or increasing. If your reactions are the same or increasing, keep writing down your feelings and thoughts. Keep going until you feel less and less of a "charge." The charge is an important signal. Keep going until you have emptied all there is to say on to the page. When you have fully expressed your feelings and thoughts, you will notice a change in your state of mind.

_____

_____

_____

_____

_____

_____

_____

_____

_____

_____

When the situation no longer feels charged, you will have brought yourself out of the *reactive zone* to a place where you can *access your constructive power.* You bring yourself to the moment Viktor Frankl describes: the moment when the work you've done to regain your presence of mind allows you to *"choose your response."* You will recognize the moment when you are "there." At that point you can identify outcomes worth having.

Reflecting on what he learned, for instance, Kyle saw his responsibility in not having doubled-checked the numbers prior to the meeting. He saw how he could now create accountability for and with his team.

Step 4: What is something you've learned?

Reflect on what you have become aware of, then determine the constructive outcome you want in the situation and/or with the person(s) involved and the actions you could take. Do you see a connection to an imbalance of your *grit* or *gravitas*?

_____

_____

_____

_____

_____

_____

_____

_____

_____

_____

Kyle wrote down the outcomes he envisioned that would generate accuracy with projections, and that would come from strengthening his relationship with his team. He then wrote down the reputation he wanted with his peers and the CEO, and the actions he needed to take to accomplish this. His actions included pulling his staff together to discuss the experience he had at the executive meeting and the outcome he wanted, pointing out each issue and what needed to change. The team worked through a plan that Kyle approved, and they understood that he would be holding them accountable. Kyle and his staff created their rules of engagement, including the kind of straight talk and honesty that would have given the accurate numbers and projections for the meeting.

Step 5: What outcomes are worth having? What actions will you take?

_____

_____

_____

_____

_____

_____

_____

_____

_____

While it may seem that it would take a lot of time to go through these steps, it winds up taking only a short time—short in comparison to the time and energy it takes to deal with the residual damage if the situation goes unchecked.

Here are the critical tasks of *reaction management* that make the biggest difference. People are going to argue, become impatient with each other, and feel let down or offended by one another—but where to go from there that encourages resolution? A *responsible release* of a reaction following an argument, for instance, is not about lashing out in anger, hurling accusations, gossiping behind someone's back, shaming them publicly, or putting them in their place even though during a reaction you might feel like doing that! A *responsible release* is one in which, with *grace*, you look to get yourself to a place where you are more aware and have gained an understanding of what triggered your reaction. For example, you understand why you felt threatened, pressured, or hopeless. You can identify your emotions and triggers without judging yourself. This helps to restore your equanimity and your presence of mind.

Train yourself to recognize when you are in the *reactive zone* so you can regain your objectivity and *presence of mind* before you do or say anything further. Train yourself to take effective measures to resolve what triggered the reaction. Train yourself to use the skills and qualities of *grace* to modulate imbalances in your *grit* and *gravitas*. Leaders who aren't inclined to do this risk becoming a liability to themselves, their team, their stakeholders, and their organization as a whole. Leaders whose reactions go unchecked, whose imbalances of *grit* and *gravitas* are given free rein in fueling their reactions, damage relationships and their reputations. They generate a brand that shows that while their results are important, there are negative consequences to the drama and difficulties of their behavior in getting to the desired results.

The skills of *reaction management* are the keys to the kingdom. For leadership there is nothing more important than dominion over how you behave day to day, and how you behave when things are at their worst.

Chapter 4

THE SECOND PILLAR OF GRACE: RELATIONSHIP INTELLIGENCE

The second pillar of *grace* is *relationship intelligence*. *Relationship intelligence* begins with your awareness of the relationship you have with yourself. The way you *relate* to yourself directly influences how you *relate* to others. And how the people you lead relate to one another has more to do with your level of self-awareness than you may realize. Something of great value takes place when you maximize your ability to relate to yourself and others through your *constructive power*. It turns out that what holds purpose and meaning for you—what we call your *highest leadership aspirations*—are an essential part of your *internal bearings*. This is your inner compass that you can use to navigate toward your evolution as a leader.

But first, given that we all have our foibles and flaws, we need to make it safe to see where our behaviors, approaches, the quality of how we relate to ourselves and how we connect with others, and our demeanor are lacking the considerable benefits our constructive power makes possible. For instance, the more you increase your ability to evaluate and adjust the imbalances in your *grit* and *gravitas,* the more aware you become of how they have been getting in your way. You will more easily identify patterns that aren't working for you. Understanding your reactions and patterns allows you to press the "edit/undo" button and replace the patterns that don't work for you.

In the pages that follow, you'll find examples of leaders who have gone through the process of identifying how they were getting in their own way, how they came to understand the negative patterns of their *grit* and their *gravitas*, and how they found the words to define their internal leadership bearings.

Our first example is Robert, a leader who did not get a role he very much wanted. Our second example, Stan, is someone who was elevated to a global position with senior VP status. Our third is Anna, who struggled with inequities she encountered in her organization.

ROBERT'S STORY

Robert, a regional director for a telecommunications company, was responsible for operations and sales for his part of the business. He actively pursued coaching to develop himself as a more effective leader. As part of his work on his leadership skills, he took the opportunity to consider his grit and his gravitas; he reviewed his current approaches, behaviors, connection with people, and his demeanor—for instance, his pattern of coming across as overconfident and self-assured. To understand the impact he was currently having as a leader, Robert reviewed the definitions of grit and gravitas and took notes regarding the times he saw himself behaving with either too much or too little grit and the times he behaved with too much or too little gravitas. He also included the feedback and advice he obtained from a previous 360 assessment from his manager, peers, and the people he led. He tied this information to what he was seeing about his grit and his gravitas.

Reflecting in this way led him to become more aware of his strengths and re-energize his desire to have a more senior executive role. But before he had taken steps to integrate what he was learning, he was presented with an opportunity. The CEO of the company, having identified Robert as a person with valuable talent and leadership skills, tapped him as a strong candidate for a position that had opened on the senior leadership team. Requested to interview as the lead candidate for this position, Robert felt certain he would be chosen. However, in his certainty that this would be easy, he reverted to his pattern of overconfidence. This came through in the three interviews he faced with the CEO, the Human Resources SVP, and a seasoned senior leadership team member. During the interviews, Robert's pattern of being overly self-assured was perceived as lacking thoughtfulness and depth. He came across to the interviewers as arrogant. The consensus of the three executives was that his answers seemed superficial, and his demeanor lacked the qualities they needed as a member of the senior leadership team. The CEO chose someone else for the role.

Discouraged and disheartened, Robert wrestled with his reactions and emotions. At first the options he saw were either fight or flight in nature: He considered leaving the company, he wrestled with his anger and disappointment with the sense he'd been treated unfairly, and he viewed the chosen candidate as having less merit than himself.

This initial reaction was followed by a period of trying to better understand what had led him to lose this opportunity he very much wanted. Taking responsibility for what had occurred, Robert came to realize that by relying on his sense of overconfidence he had derailed this opportunity.

For Robert, this experience was an important wake-up call. He decided that instead of leaving the company where he had been very successful, he would work to turn things around in his current role. He turned his efforts toward integrating the skills and qualities of grace into his leadership. As part of this work, he began with the following question: What kind of leader is it important for me to be? Why does this matter? In answering these questions, Robert reflected on leaders he had admired over the years.

He looked very carefully at what had impressed him about how they led, including their approaches, their behaviors, the quality of their connection with people, and what he'd noticed about their demeanor. He asked himself what kind of influence he wanted to be able to have should another opportunity to join the senior leadership team become available to him. He considered the qualities that would allow him to be a more positive influence with his peers and the people he leads. He looked at changes he could make that would allow him to be a more effective leader when challenges and difficult problems arose.

Robert took the opportunity to make important changes in his leadership, a decision not every leader would choose to make. But when a leader does make this choice, what motivates him or her to do so? Some of the motivations that have been shared with us are included in the following: For some, it is a wake-up call of one sort or another; for others, it may start out with wanting to be a part of, or a catalyst for, something that makes for a more meaningful and fulfilling life. Still others have a sense that they want greater peace of mind and the ability to empower themselves in the face of troubling situations they are not in control of. But at a moment of choice there is always a kind of coming to terms with their situation, a deeper reflection that results in a leader's very personal answers to essential questions.

Relationship intelligence begins with the way you relate to yourself, which directly influences how you relate to others. In Robert's case, in addition to what he discovered from the interviews, he considered his leadership in general, facing his foibles and flaws as a leader. He recognized imbalances where too much *grit* and *gravitas* on his part obscured his perspective when it came to the opportunity to have the kind of impact he'd like to have.

What comes to mind for you? Are there situations where the imbalance of too much *grit* is having a negative impact and getting in your way?

If so, how? What are you noticing? What feedback have you received?

_____

_____

_____

_____

_____

_____

_____

Are there imbalances where you notice that too much *gravitas* is having a negative effect and is getting in your way?

If so, how? What are you noticing? What feedback have you received?

_____

_____

_____

_____

_____

_____

_____

Sometimes a painful situation acts as a catalyst for our development. Sometimes, as in the story of Stan below, it is an inclination, a personal drive to improve that is the catalyst. There is honor in the efforts to develop ourselves regardless of the trigger that inspires us to do so.

STAN'S STORY

Stan had the opportunity to move from a VP level leader of a single division to a larger global role at the Senior VP level. While Robert's situation was driven by a failure to achieve an important goal, Stan had a natural inclination toward the idea of becoming exemplary as a leader. His new role had a wider scope of leadership responsibility. Stan became responsible for three new divisions with sites throughout North America, Europe, Latin America, and Asia, tripling the number of direct reports under his watch.

Stan considered his default patterns; he looked at them in light of what would be expected of him in this new role and environment. He saw that it would require him to develop additional leadership skills, skills that would allow him to address the complexities and design structures that would be needed to achieve results. Further, Stan identified additional leadership skills he would need to interface successfully with the various microcultures involved in this complex environment.

Working together with us, as he prepared for this new role, he asked himself questions such as: "What will this new role require of me as a leader? What skills will I need?"

Addressing his default patterns and the imbalances of his grit and gravitas, Stan became aware of the tendencies he had that could be a problem in his new role. For example, he recognized an imbalance in his gravitas that related to the following: Although he saw himself as humble and it wasn't his intent, someone with gravitas in their profession can sometimes be perceived as intimidating and unapproachable because of their considerable knowledge or ability. They may lack the skills that would allow them to be more connected and at ease in collaborating with their teammates and colleagues. Stan recognized that he had a pattern of expressing his opinions and experiences in ways that didn't allow for more collaborative discussions. In his desire to ensure his peers and employees understood everything including all possible risks,

Stan came across in a "communicating to send, not receive" way that didn't allow for dialogue. Seeing this, he was inspired to reconsider a better way to interact with his teams in his new role.

In his reflections, Stan saw other examples of default patterns, such as his reluctance to ask for support. Part of grit is a leader's comfort level with their power, which includes the ability to delegate and invite collaboration and support. He recognized that this imbalance in his grit was motivated by his concern for not imposing on anyone. This is one of the ways leaders manifest their discomfort with power.

Stan also recognized that he had an aversion to systematic approaches—approaches that are more organized and methodical than his current ones. As he considered the meaning he placed behind the idea of flexibility, he saw how he had been confused about the idea that structures get in the way of being flexible. Stan realized that flexibility needs to coexist with organization and structure; it wasn't a matter of one or the other. He also saw how the unintended consequences of his default pattern could interfere with efficiency, effectiveness, and progress in how he leads. Stan considered proactive ways to correct these imbalances in his grit, learning that he can still be flexible in his thought process while setting up systems that will ensure consistency and cross-functionally coordinated efforts.

Knowing he wanted to be exemplary, Stan faced his foibles and flaws so he could determine the best development plan for himself as a leader. Beginning this process, he reflected on the question: "What kind of leader is it important for me to be, and why?" He reflected on the leaders he had admired over the years. He looked very carefully at what had impressed him about how they led, what he observed in their approaches, their behaviors, the quality of their connection with people, and their demeanor. He asked himself what kind of impact he wanted to be able to have with his new stakeholders, and with the people he would now lead. He considered what would allow

THE SECOND PILLAR OF GRACE: RELATIONSHIP INTELLIGENCE

him to be an exemplary leader when there were challenges and when there were hard problems to solve. What would he need to pay attention to, to increase his reaction management skills and his relationship intelligence?

As you consider Stan's story, what thoughts come to mind?

_____

_____

_____

_____

_____

_____

_____

_____

When you are moving to a new role, or your responsibilities and reach of your impact are increasing, what are a couple of things you would like to address and improve?

_____

_____

_____

_____

_____

_____

_____

What comes to mind for you in terms of new opportunities or a new role? Are there situations where the imbalance of too much or too little *grit* or too much or too little *gravitas* could impede your effectiveness in your new role?

If so, what are you becoming aware of?

_____

_____

_____

_____

_____

_____

_____

ANNA'S STORY

Anna and William were partners in a financial services firm they had started together. Their firm was acquired by a larger global financial services corporation. One of the persistent challenges Anna faced in the new larger firm was what appeared to be an exclusive "good old boys club." One example is how this group of men shared among themselves the larger client opportunities that arose. Notwithstanding Anna's gravitas and her considerable professional competence and expertise, these client opportunities were not extended to her. Bringing this dilemma to William's attention did nothing to alleviate the situation. He was unable to empathize with her; he was enjoying this advantage he had in the new culture, and in their discussions together he defended the rationale for why the clients were offered to him. He was happy with the recognition and status he had gained, along with the bonus and benefits that came with it at year end.

Speaking to William only added to the frustration and stress Anna was experiencing. She realized she could not turn to William to help her resolve the situation as she might have in the past. The culture was one that permitted the kind of behavior Anna was up against; not wanting to leave her position, Anna saw the need to find another way to resolve her stress and frustration.

As we worked together, Anna saw that she had choices in the matter. She took an honest look at the frustration, resentment, and anger she had been feeling over the situation and the cost to her energy and well-being; she realized the extensive inequity of the situation and the disempowering effect it was having on her life. Fighting the situation would continue to be exhausting. It would place her in an adversarial position and detract from her ability to focus and build value for her clients.

Taking stock of it all at this important time in her life, she considered her options and made a decision to remain with the firm. She assessed and evaluated the results she had achieved year after year; she got in touch with the extraordinary commitment she had to her clients and their success; and she recognized in no uncertain terms how dedicated she was—and had been throughout her career. Seeing all of this, she decided to forge her own path forward. She put into words her *highest leadership aspirations*, and once her *internal bearings* were in place, she was able to harness the *constructive power of grace* for herself. She was able to face the inequities she'd been dealing with more objectively without her *grit* being filled with bitterness and resentment. She let go of the frustration and anger and took back her power; she felt empowered by recognizing her own value—not in an arrogant way but in a grounded and meaningful way. She was able to understand and own the depth and breadth of her gravitas with a deeper level of respect from within herself. She began to focus her energies in a different way.

Keeping her *internal bearings* present, Anna was able to re-energize and empower herself. No longer disempowered by the reactions she had to the built-in biases of the culture, her grasp of her *higher aspirations* shifted the way she focused and utilized her energy and expertise. Her stress levels decreased, her results increased and, with the changes that were reflected in her approaches, behaviors, the quality of her connection with people, and her demeanor, her presence in the organization began to be recognized and appreciated in new and important ways.

As you consider Anna's challenges, do any situations come to mind that you or someone else have experienced? How could too much or too little *grit* or *gravitas* get in the way? How could the constructive power of *grace* add power to yours or their *grit* and *gravitas*?

_____

_____

_____

_____

_____

_____

_____

_____

Part of evolving as a leader is connecting with our higher self, our higher aspirations, the better angels of our nature, to clarify and determine what we can reach for within ourselves and ask of ourselves.

It is important to keep your internal bearings clear and present. Let's explore finding the words that hold meaning for you.

The internal bearings process allows you to re-define the kind of leader it is important to you to be. The following are prompts to help you define your internal bearings and arrive at the heart of the matter for yourself. You will become clearer about your aspirations and your values and learn how to elevate emotional operating states.

Step 1: Defining my internal bearings.

Your highest leadership aspirations are distinct from your personal goals. Take a moment to consider your ambitions alongside your highest leadership aspirations.

There is a clear relationship between your "ambitions" and your "higher aspirations." Your ambitions will reflect your goals: what you are working to achieve for yourself. They relate to factors such as your status in the organization, which can include goals such as making partner or joining the executive team. Your ambitions also can include your financial goals and some combination of salary and bonus that lets you know you are hitting the mark of what you've set out to achieve. In this exercise you are looking for your highest leadership aspirations: your values—the things that are of the greatest importance to you in the way you aspire to live, work, and lead. You are putting into words what you want to give, share, and contribute to others.

Use this important time with yourself to reflect on the following questions that help you connect with your highest leadership aspirations:

Who are the leaders I admire? What behaviors and qualities am I drawn to in their leadership?

_____

_____

_____

_____

_____

_____

_____

_____

_____

_____

The answers you are looking for reflect your highest aspirations for yourself as a leader. When you think about the leaders you've admired and the leaders who've inspired you how would you describe the qualities you admire in their character? In the quality of their connection with people? What do you admire about their impact on people?

_____

_____

_____

_____

_____

_____

_____

_____

_____

What approaches and behaviors impressed you? What did you observe that you respected and admired?

_____

_____

_____

_____

_____

_____

_____

_____

_____

Your highest leadership aspirations are a result of reflections that help you define *your higher purpose and calling as a leader.* They reflect what holds meaning for you in answering the question: *What kind of leader is it important for me to be and why?* The work of clarifying your highest aspirations will bring you in touch with what matters to you most, arriving at the heart of the matter for yourself. Your highest aspirations give you essential guidelines for your life and are the defining element of your internal bearings.

As a leader, what matters to me? What meaningful contributions would I most want to provide for the people I have the opportunity, or will soon have the opportunity, to lead?

_____

_____

_____

_____

_____

_____

_____

_____

_____

_____

What is my ideal for my leadership that is worth reaching for? What values and qualities distinguish my ideal?

_____

_____

_____

_____

_____

_____

_____

_____

_____

_____

What legacy would I most like to leave? What would I like to be remembered for?

_____

_____

_____

_____

_____

_____

_____

_____

_____

_____

Some useful things to consider: Everyone can find their own way of putting their aspirations into words. Once clarified, your words will hold great energy and meaning. As you find the words that best express your aspirations, you will have arrived at the heart of the matter for yourself; you will have captured what holds the greatest meaning for you at this important time in your life.

As you write down your aspirations, be conscious of allowing this to be a creative process, a chance to connect with the heart of what matters to you. Give yourself some room to expand your ideas without your internal criticizer taking over and being in charge. Take time to reflect, for several days if necessary. Start with an initial draft of your ideas. At first you may find yourself listing activities. Take a break for a few minutes and then return to what you have written.

If you listed activities, ask yourself: What do I aspire to that will lead me to these choices and actions?

_____

_____

_____

_____

_____

_____

_____

_____

The following are some examples of aspirations our clients have identified:

- To keep our mission present so that we are, as a team, able to be inspired by how, both individually and collectively, we are making our vision come to life in the day to day of our work and over the long term.

- As a leader, I am committed to bringing out the best from the members of my team. I want to be known as a leader who generates group trust, alignment, and collaboration. I want to shift my tendency to work with individuals and become adept at getting the best performance from and with the team.

- To engage with my direct reports in ways that inspire their energy and engagement by not solving their problems for them, as I have done in the past. Instead, I strengthen my ability to invite their ideas and solutions; I express my confidence in their abilities to solve, innovate, and execute effectively.

- To continuously pursue the improvement of my strategic thinking by learning through my experiences—both successes and challenges—and by taking responsible risks that elevate my wisdom and choices as a leader.

- To be attentive to providing valuable guidance and strategic advice I can offer the organization by communicating with my stakeholders in a way that is relatable, commercially reasonable, creative, forward-thinking, and based on high integrity.

- To develop a greater strength in recognizing and developing talent. As a leader, I'm committed to helping the organization continue to evolve and stay ahead of the competition. I will identify and develop the next generation of leaders that will be seen as part of the "commercial team" and as "true partners."

When you are reading another's leadership aspirations, remember that they hold meaning and energy for their author. By identifying your highest leadership aspirations, you will find you are inspired and energized by your words. The positive energy and inspiration you feel confirm that you have gotten to the heart of what matters to you as a leader.

Chapter 5

RELATIONSHIP INTELLIGENCE: LEADERSHIP & THE SOCIAL BRAIN

The impact you have as a leader is the determining factor of the culture you generate, whether you are leading the entire organization, a division, a geographic territory, or a project team. Having completed your work in Chapter 4 of this workbook, you have begun to define your highest leadership aspirations and create the foundation of your internal bearings. The key to your evolution as a leader is that by keeping your internal bearings present and leading from them, your leadership is going to evolve.

Many studies of brain science emerging over recent years have proven that the human brain is a social organ, and that our physiological and neurological reactions are shaped by our social interactions. Let's consider the relationship intelligence offered to us through the social brain as it affects the dynamics taking place in social interactions in organizational settings. The social brain is a source of invisible cues when social interactions are taking place. Recent scientific discoveries find that in the brain the amygdala is not just on the lookout for danger. It also searches for cues and clues that help us in building our social connections. As a leader, it is important to pay special attention to the evidence that social bonds matter more than we might realize.

The most important element for any one of us to have a happy and fulfilling life rests on the nature, quality, and reliability of our relationships. The good life, it turns out, according to a study Harvard has done—the Harvard Study of Adult Development—is built through cultivating and sustaining good relationships. Toxic relationships are bad for one's health, even worse than divorce. Consider that people spend a tremendous amount of their lives at work. As a leader, do you bring people together ways that are meaningful? Every day you have the opportunity to ensure that people's lives are made better by virtue of the culture you create and the way your approaches, behaviors, the quality of your connection with people, and your demeanor can foster a constructive influence on the quality of relationships at work.

Make a few notes for yourself about what you are doing, or what you can start doing, to foster a meaningful environment for those you lead and constructively influence the quality of relationships with your team:

_____

_____

_____

_____

_____

_____

_____

As you come to understand the social dynamics going on within the brain, you can more effectively engage your employees' best talents, support their collaborative synergy and teamwork, and use the relationship intelligence you are gaining to ensure that the people you lead feel considered, respected, and safe.

As we saw with reaction management in Chapter 3, when we are having a reaction, we can notice our amygdala is signaling a threat. We can notice the fight or flight reaction that has been triggered. We can pause and identify the emotion we are experiencing, such as embarrassment, anger, frustration, or disappointment; we can recognize the need being thwarted or blocked, such as the need for a teammate's cooperation when they failed to follow through as promised, or the disappointment when we learn we cannot trust someone we thought we could rely on. We can recognize the initial reactive thoughts about who is right or wrong or who is to blame but not stop there. We can look a little deeper; we can understand more clearly and more compassionately why we felt upset. We may not be able to change what occurred, but we can, as we gain greater self-awareness, empower ourselves in handling and resolving the situation at hand.

As a leader, you can draw on your constructive power to manage the impact of your reactions, restore your presence of mind, and identify actions that lead to constructive outcomes. You can also guide your team with this knowledge in mind. You can support your team to constructively resolve challenging situations. You can clearly define rules of engagement and provide a sense of belonging, empowerment, trust, and alignment your team can rely on.

Why does this matter to the achievement of outcomes you are committed to? Make some notes for yourself below: what are you already doing, what would you like to start doing, and what would you like to stop doing?

_____

_____

_____

_____

_____

_____

_____

The social brain and psychological safety

> *A critical part of relationship intelligence is the ability to create psychological safety for and with the people you lead...*

Let's examine one of the key elements for putting relationship intelligence into action, creating the conditions for psychological safety.

Why is it important for a leader to know how to provide psychological safety? Here are a couple of reasons to consider: When leaders provide psychological safety, they are providing a safety net; one that helps employees face and deal with the emotional uncertainties and anxieties of change. Providing psychological safety is a critical part of how and why a leader earns people's trust, of how and why people feel they and their contributions matter.

Think of a leader you felt or feel comfortable with when speaking up. What do you notice about this leader? What makes it comfortable to bring up your ideas or concerns?

_____

_____

_____

_____

_____

_____

_____

_____

Next, think of a leader around whom you would hesitate to speak out or share your opinion. What is it that makes you hesitate to speak? The focus of this question is about the role *leaders* have in making it psychologically safe for people to contribute their ideas and concerns. This is different than someone not speaking up due to a lack of self-confidence.

_____

_____

_____

_____

_____

_____

_____

We have seen many leaders with considerable *gravitas*—deep knowledge in their field—who value their own thoughts and opinions, which is important, but express their thoughts and opinions in ways that discourage a two-way discussion. They devalue the thoughts and perspectives of the people on their team. Often these leaders have a habit of correcting and putting down team members who speak up; this establishes a pattern that it is not safe. Psychological safety is critical for the establishment of trust in a group or organization.

The BETA Model

The constructive power of *grace* helps leaders meet the needs of the social brain, the social needs of the people they lead. For that purpose, we turn now to the BETA Model. Use this model as a guide to help understand the social needs of groups and teams and to generate the social conditions that translate into Belonging, Empowerment, Trust, and Alignment. Based on research of the social brain and human needs at work, this model touches on specific dynamics that can result in cultures that invite people to be and do their best, to feel a sense of being part of something meaningful and important that makes them feel, as is mentioned in the book, *"we are close, we are safe, we share a future."* Let's look at the BETA Model and see how the constructive power of *grace* provides for the social brain's needs and the conditions that foster an environment where cooperation and collaboration lead to high performance.

How to use the BETA Model to diagnose

Belonging, Empowerment, Trust, and Alignment are foundational conditions for high performing teams. When issues and problems arise with your team, how can you zero in on the root causes of the matter? Many of the root causes of team dysfunction can be attributed to one or more of the elements within the BETA Model. It is structured to help you identify areas of compromise affecting your team's productivity, engagement, and progress. Here is the model itself, followed by steps that can serve as a guide in using the model:

BETA MODEL

The social brain: meaningful engagement, unlocking potential, psychological safety...

Belonging	Empowerment	Trust	Alignment
CREATING THE CONDITIONS FOR SHARED MEANING AND PURPOSE	CREATING THE CONDITIONS FOR LEVERAGING POTENTIAL, AND ENGAGEMENT	CREATING THE CONDITIONS FOR PSYCHOLOGICAL SAFETY	CREATING THE CONDITIONS FOR MAKING SENSE OF THINGS TOGETHER
Inclusion and acceptance	Non-judgmental listening and asking constructive questions that facilitates resolution of challenges	Generous listening and understanding neutralizing negativity	Constructive focus, attention, and efforts, "Can do", "We'll figure this out" approaches
Keeping the door open; being available in general on a consistent basis	Recognizing each team member's value and importance in achieving goals	Being trustworthy and dependable, keeping promises	All-in regarding the team's shared vision, mission and purpose
Approaches that take social needs into consideration	Recognizing and developing the potential, skills, and talent of the people on the team	Fairness with due consideration for differences, diversity, and individual needs.	Flexibility, cooperation, and a spirit of collaborative partnering in evaluating and taking risks
A purpose and mission that people are proud to be a part of	Conflict and/or failure handled in a constructive way; remembering that when things go wrong, we can learn from them	Honesty, integrity, authenticity, and sincerity	Clearly defined direction, goals and responsibilities
Respect and regard for other's perspectives	Ensuring each member of the team has the resources needed to succeed	Compassion for vulnerabilities, including one's own	Putting agreed upon measures and accountabilities in place
All for one, one for all: Shared appreciation for the team's contributions and accomplishments	Advocacy and support team members where and when it matters	Support, cooperation, compromise and forgiveness	Approaching team challenges constructively; rules of engagement and shared values
Keeping vision, mission, and purpose present and active	Bringing objectivity and empathy to disagreements and disruptions	Owning one's responsibility and expressing apology	Putting platforms, structures, resources in place to ensure success

www.gritgracegravitas.com

Thinking about your team, recall a current challenging situation:

1. Consider the situation your team is facing. Scan each column of the BETA Model to help you identify elements that may be contributing to the situation. For instance, are cooperation and communication breaking down? Are there unresolved issues between members of your team?

_____

_____

_____

_____

_____

_____

_____

The questions below will further clarify each element you've identified. For example, look at the conditions for:

Belonging in column one: For example, is someone on your team feeling out of the loop or not included?

_____

_____

_____

_____

_____

_____

_____

Empowerment in column two: For example, does someone on your team lack the resources they need?

_____

_____

_____

_____

_____

_____

Trust in column three: For example, is someone on your team feeling that the work is not being handled fairly or that they're not receiving due consideration for their contribution?

_____

_____

_____

_____

_____

_____

Alignment in column four: For example, is someone on your team lacking clear direction, goals, or responsibilities?

_____

_____

_____

_____

_____

_____

Check in with yourself: Write down what comes to mind as you consider the following:

2. Am I providing the conditions for Belonging, Empowerment, Trust, and Alignment? For example:

Have I been available? What do I notice about this? Is there something I could improve?

_____

_____

_____

_____

_____

_____

_____

_____

_____

_____

Am I listening generously and objectively? Is there something I could do a better job of, for instance, in how I listen?

_____

_____

_____

_____

_____

_____

_____

_____

_____

_____

Am I creating psychological safety? What measures on my part could improve this?

_____

_____

_____

_____

_____

_____

_____

Am I being clear in how I give directions and set expectations? If not, what measures could I take towards doing a better job with this?

_____

_____

_____

_____

_____

_____

_____

3. Take a few minutes with yourself to consider the following questions:

What further actions and steps would help to address and improve the elements I've identified?

_____

_____

_____

_____

_____

_____

What will I do differently to create the conditions for psychological safety and generate honest dialogue with my team members?

_____

_____

_____

_____

_____

_____

_____

_____

What are some optimal outcomes to the issues I've identified, and what constructive approaches can I take to get us there?

_____

_____

_____

_____

_____

_____

_____

_____

As you become familiar with the aspects of the BETA Model, you will begin to see how best to put these distinctions into action.

AMBER'S STORY

Amber interviewed for the position of vice president to lead a team. This team had gone through significant problems with the leader Amber was replacing. Having been hired for the role, Amber took steps in talking with HR to gain an in-depth understanding of each of her direct reports. She was able to gather important perspectives and information and understand what the last few years had been like for each person on her team.

Based on this helpful information, Amber recognized how building Trust would serve the team she was about to inherit. To create the conditions for psychological safety, she saw that when she had an opportunity to speak in person with her direct reports, it would be important to listen in a way that would help her gain understanding and be able to neutralize any negativity that had developed over the prior years.

Amber saw the importance of creating the conditions for Empowerment that would allow her to develop the potential of each team member and inspire their engagement. As Amber shared the approaches she took in getting started with her team, she shared the following:

"I felt it was important to keep in mind that I came from outside the system to lead people who had been through a tough couple of years. I knew it was important to me not to just 'barge in.' I took time with each of them to talk about their expectations and hesitations and understand what they were looking for in a leader. They had concerns such as: Would I be able to understand the work that they did? How would I deal with the fact that they didn't feel like a team? They were on the lookout to see what I did: Would I listen first or just change things? How would I represent them to the higher levels of leadership within the organization? Was I a leader who would value each of them? Could they trust me?"

"Almost immediately, they let me know that their interactions with me were very different from the way they had been dealt with over the last few years. I took time to meet with each of them individually as well as together, and I asked them to tell me: 'What do you do in your role? Tell me about it.' And then I shared some of my strengths and experiences with them and what I could provide. Then I asked: 'What do you need from me? What would add value coming from me?' One of my direct reports let me know that she cared about having interesting work; she wanted to take on projects that offered her a challenge and a chance to grow. Later she shared with me that through these conversations she felt like she was empowered to grow and contribute for the first time in a long time. I felt really good about that."

Amber took the risk of being vulnerable with her team.

"In all the conversations I had with my team I found myself in a moment when I took a big risk. I said to my team, 'There is a lot you know that I don't. I will do the best I can, but I will make mistakes. Please have patience with me. I want us to be a team.' Somehow showing my own vulnerability helped my team members feel safe in sharing their feelings with me. I did let them know that, as a leader, I was in charge... I told them: 'I want, and I value, your perspectives. At the end of the day, you can count on me to make the decisions.'"

Whether you are starting your first leadership opportunity or are a seasoned leader in your field, your influence and impact can help to transform a dysfunctional team culture and help to generate the conditions in which team members feel a sense of Belonging, Empowerment, Trust, and Alignment. Your approaches and behaviors toward your team, and the quality of your connection with them, as well as your demeanor, make the defining difference in members of your team knowing they are valued, are able to feel inspired and engaged with you and each other, and are motivated toward a shared purpose and meaningful goals.

What comes to mind when you consider that Amber recognized the importance of understanding the needs of her direct reports? What have you been able to clarify regarding the needs of those who report to you?

_____

_____

_____

_____

_____

_____

_____

_____

_____

What thoughts do you have about the importance of Amber conveying consideration, respect, empathy, and compassion toward those she led? What consequences follow when this is missing?

_____

_____

_____

_____

_____

_____

_____

_____

_____

What thoughts come to mind regarding Amber having taken the risk of being vulnerable with her team?

_____

_____

_____

_____

_____

_____

_____

_____

_____

As a leader, in light of what you are becoming aware of with the BETA Model, what have you done, or what could you do now, to have your team trust that you have their backs, to have them know that they are valued, and that their needs are being considered?

_____

_____

_____

_____

_____

_____

_____

_____

_____

_____

When it comes to establishing psychological safety in a way that translates into a sense of belonging, research shows the following: *"A mere hint of belonging is not enough; one or two signals are not enough. We are built to require lots of signaling, over and over. This is why a sense of belonging is easy to destroy and hard to build"* (Coyle, 2018).

What steps are you taking, or what steps could you now take, that establish and sustain psychological safety?

_____

_____

_____

_____

_____

_____

_____

What actions come to mind as you consider creating a sense of belonging with your team? How can a sense of being a part of something meaningful and inspiring be established in a sustainable way with your team?

_____

_____

_____

_____

_____

_____

_____

WAYNE'S STORY

Promoted to a vice president position within a large construction company, Wayne successfully advanced up the career ladder. His success was based on his knowledge, skills, and experience with all facets of construction, along with a prowess for bringing in sales. Considered smart and thoughtful with sound opinions and a thorough understanding of the market, Wayne and his contributions were highly valuable. He was offered his VP position without having had leadership experience.

After Wayne had a 360 assessment with his key stakeholders, his assessment feedback indicated some areas for development including his tendency to be disorganized and resistant to using systematic approaches. Wayne's approach to getting things done was, in his words, "overly adaptable and flexible," which reflected an imbalance of too little grit; it left his stakeholders with a lack of confidence and certainty. Another imbalance in his grit was how he avoided confrontations and giving difficult feedback to others when needed. Wayne's stakeholders were left with concerns about his lack of ability to hold his followers to account.

He decided to focus his development plan on building a high performing team under his leadership. Using the BETA Model, Wayne realized that his focus on his production would have to shift to facilitating the productivity of others. Since he preferred maintaining harmony in relationships, he was hesitant to let others know when they didn't meet his expectations. In building Trust, Wayne wanted his direct reports to feel a sense of psychological safety and Belonging. He looked at how he could set the conditions for giving and receiving feedback, fostering healthy conflict, and increasing engagement, as well as taking calculated risks. By setting the conditions for Empowerment, he would be better able to promote skill development. He saw how developing the conditions for the team's Alignment would help him to provide supporting processes and structures, along with accountability for results.

Wayne sat in on some of the team meetings to observe the performance and characteristics of those who would be reporting to him. He also asked the former team leader and other stakeholders of the team about their perceptions of the team's performance. In doing so, he learned that there was an inconsistency in being responsive to stakeholder requests and concerns. He could also see that each direct report tended toward operating independently rather than as a team.

Another part of Wayne's strategy was to foster a connection with his team members; he decided to meet with his direct reports one on one to get to know them better, understand what motivated them, and learn what they found challenging both in their roles and within the group. One of his strengths was listening to understand, which, as described in the BETA Model, is an element of setting the conditions for Trust. With confidence, Wayne asked questions and shared some of his own experiences. One of the practical insights Wayne came away with from his one-on-one discussions was that his team would value weekly meetings with clear agendas.

How does a leader inspire individuals who are used to operating independently and transform them from individuals to members of a team? To this end, Wayne put a great deal of thought into his first kick-off team meeting, organizing an agenda that would build Trust.

Wayne asked them to write down one simple action—something they could practice with one another—that would increase their mutual trust throughout the coming month. He provided an example that they could use in making their commitment or customize one of their own. His example was: "When an issue with a team member arises, instead of listening only to my own assumptions and defaulting to my habit of working independently, I will ask questions to better connect and understand others' perspectives and ideas."

Difficulty holding people to account was one of the imbalances Wayne wanted to address in his development. In correcting this imbalance in his *grit*, he thought of ways to make accountability more user-friendly.

For the planned meeting the following month, Wayne sent the group an agenda, which included the critical topic of customer service. He began with a lively team exercise by requesting each team member to reflect on times they had a positive experience with a client service representative and times when they had a negative experience. As Wayne worked on setting the conditions for Alignment, the discussion prompted the team to make sense of things together. They looked at the lack of structure, processes, and practices in the department, and they saw the benefits they could have in creating them.

Wayne then facilitated a team discussion to arrive at a group vision, one that would build a strong reputation with their stakeholders. The team then looked at ways to structure consistent approaches. They brainstormed measures of success for driving the consistency of customer service. Wayne observed the increase in energy that everyone, including himself, was feeling.

He finished the meeting with the same request as the first meeting, for a simple individual commitment to a behavior that would serve to improve their customer service during the coming month, one that could become sustainable as a habit. Wayne requested they each choose a different accountability buddy than they had before to provide them with constructive support and feedback at least once during the month. The consistency of supporting each other in this way and their growing appreciation for each other's roles and efforts contributed in a positive way to his team feeling a sense of inclusion and Belonging.

As Wayne integrated constructive power into his *grit* and *gravitas*, he also began to help his team develop their ability to use their constructive power with each other.

As you develop and evolve as a leader, your ability to develop others and help them evolve increases. You may find some similarities with Wayne's imbalances, or as you identify your own, they might be quite different. Either way, the BETA Model will be a faithful guide in building the conditions for Belonging, Empowerment, Trust, and Alignment with your team. Use the following questions to guide your thought process:

A. Do you struggle with having difficult conversations and holding people to account? What happens? How does this impact your emotional state and relationship with members of your team?

_____

_____

_____

_____

_____

_____

_____

_____

Or, **B.**, do you have difficult conversations where you hold people to account in ways that result in having a negative, rather than a constructive, impact and outcome?

_____

_____

_____

_____

_____

_____

_____

_____

Wayne inspired the individuals who were used to operating independently to come together as a team. How do you or would you go about doing that with your team?

_____

_____

_____

_____

_____

_____

_____

The element of trust is critical here. How do you build trust with your team? What builds trust? What erodes trust?

_____

_____

_____

_____

_____

_____

_____

Using the BETA Model to elevate emotional states

An emotional state of mind can be negative, neutral, or positive. When people do not feel a sense of Belonging, Empowerment, Trust, or Alignment, their emotional state will be affected. Each member of the team could have a different reaction based on unmet BETA needs.

The elevation of an emotional state of mind happens when social issues and concerns are understood, addressed, and resolved.

A trusted leader can lean in to his or her constructive power by asking questions with a sincere desire to understand through their empathy and compassion. Try the following process:

Address and acknowledge that there is an issue. For instance, you could say: *"We seem to be out of Alignment, and I want us to get back on track. What do you think has taken us out of Alignment with each other?"*

Establish a condition for attentive listening. Set a ground rule to have each person share their perspective completely before another takes their turn in sharing their perspective.

After each person has an opportunity to fully express their concerns, mirror back what you have heard to be sure you've got the essence of what they are expressing, and ensure they know you've understood their perspective.

Ask each person: "Is there anything else? Am I missing anything?"

Thank them for taking the risk of being honest.

Chapter 6

THE IMPACT OF LEADERSHIP ON CULTURE

Now let's look further into using the BETA Model to diagnose the conditions getting in the way of constructive team dynamics and broaden our view to include some of the ways a leader's role impacts organizational culture; let's look more closely at how executive presence impacts people, performance, and outcomes.

As a leader, every challenge you face with your team is an opportunity to reinforce the social contract you're building into the culture; how you deal with each challenge reinforces values in action.

1. **Choose a situation you are currently facing with your team.**

Consider the situation the team is facing. Scan each column to help you identify elements that may be contributing to the situation. What might be at the core of where and why, for example, cooperation and communication are breaking down?

- Refer back to the BETA Model: As you scan the columns, which elements catch your attention?

_____

_____

_____

_____

_____

_____

_____

_____

_____

Use the BETA Model to constructively impact the quality of an organization's culture

In the BETA Model, each element serves a specific purpose, which leaders can use to create the social-emotional conditions that elevate the culture and emotional operating states of organizations and teams.

Let's review the purpose provided by each element of the BETA Model:

- **Belonging** creates the conditions for shared meaning and purpose
- **Empowerment** creates the conditions for leveraging potential and engagement
- **Trust** creates the conditions for psychological safety
- **Alignment** creates the conditions for making sense of things together

To elevate the conditions people are working inside of, as you consider each of the components of the BETA Model—the purpose of each component and the conditions each component allows for—you will be able to diagnose your situation and determine important steps you can take to resolve what is missing.

Let's begin with **Belonging.**

Belonging *creates the conditions for shared meaning and purpose.* **Below are some of the actions that help to generate the conditions for shared meaning and purpose:**

- Inclusion and acceptance
- Keeping the door open, being available in general on a consistent basis
- Approaches that take social needs into consideration
- A purpose and mission that are inspiring and meaningful, that people are proud to be a part of
- Respect and regard for others' perspectives
- All for one, one for all: shared appreciation for the team's contributions and accomplishments
- Keeping vision, mission, and purpose present and active

As you consider each element above, what actions could you take? What improvements could you make?

_____

_____

_____

_____

_____

_____

_____

_____

Empowerment *creates the conditions for leveraging potential and engagement.* **Below are some of the elements and actions to consider:**

- Non-judgmental listening, and offering constructive questions that facilitate resolution of challenges
- Recognizing each team member's value and importance in achieving goals
- Recognizing and developing the potential, skills, and talent of the people on the team
- Conflict and/or failure handled in a constructive way; remembering that when things go wrong, we can learn and regroup
- Ensuring each member of the team has the resources needed to succeed
- Advocacy for, and support of team members where and when it matters
- Bringing objectivity and empathy to disagreements and disruptions

Empowerment: As you consider each element above, what actions could you take? What improvements could you make?

_____

_____

_____

_____

_____

_____

_____

_____

_____

_____

_____

_____

_____

_____

Trust *creates the conditions for psychological safety.* **Below are some of the elements and actions that invite Trust:**

- Generous listening and understanding, valuing others' perspectives and contributions
- Neutralizing negativity
- Being trustworthy and dependable, keeping promises
- Fairness with due consideration for differences, diversity, and individual needs
- Honesty, integrity, authenticity, and sincerity
- Compassion for vulnerabilities, including one's own
- Support, cooperation, and forgiveness
- Owning one's responsibility and expressing apology

Trust: As you consider the elements above, what changes and actions would make a difference?

_____

_____

_____

_____

_____

_____

_____

_____

_____

_____

_____

_____

Alignment *creates the conditions for making sense of things together.* **Below are some of the elements and actions that serve to generate Alignment:**

- Constructive focus, attention, and efforts, along with "Can do," "We'll figure this out together" approaches
- All-in regarding the teams' shared vision, mission, and purpose
- Flexibility, cooperation, and a spirit of collaborative partnering in evaluating and taking risks
- Clearly defined direction, goals, and responsibilities
- Putting agreed upon measures and accountabilities in place
- Approaching team challenges constructively, rules of engagement and shared values
- Putting platforms, structures, resources in place to ensure success

Alignment: Make some notes for yourself as you consider the elements above. What changes and what actions could restore Alignment?

_____

_____

_____

_____

_____

_____

_____

_____

_____

_____

_____

_____

2. Take a few minutes with yourself to consider the following questions:

What additional steps would help address and resolve the elements I've identified?

_____

_____

_____

_____

_____

_____

What else can I do differently to create the conditions for psychological safety and generate honest dialogue with my team members?

_____

_____

_____

_____

_____

_____

What is an optimal outcome, and what constructive approaches can I take to get us there?

_____

_____

_____

_____

_____

_____

As you reflect on the social needs not being met, what conversations could you have to reestablish the sense of Belonging or Empowerment or Trust or Alignment that has become compromised? For example:

Maybe a member of your team expressed they've felt excluded from important conversations or perhaps several team members feel they are overburdened by their workload and lack sufficient resources they need to accomplish their goals.

What measures could you take to resolve these issues? How could you help increase their sense of being more empowered? For example, let's suppose ideal resources are unavailable right now. Thinking constructively, is there a way of sharing the workload that both pulls people together and lessens the burden each is feeling? Does acknowledging the situations people are up against help? For example, *I know resources are not available right now; how can we lessen the burden on ourselves even though we can't increase resources right now?*

_____

_____

_____

_____

_____

_____

_____

_____

_____

_____

_____

_____

_____

When you constructively address issues together with your team, the emotional operating state of yourself and those you lead will elevate. Although there may be no immediate way to provide the necessary resources, when people feel heard, empowered, and respected, there is an opening to work through issues and concerns together in ways that generate understanding and increase Belonging, Empowerment, Trust, and Alignment.

When social issues are allowed to remain unresolved, your team is operating in a negative emotional state. When this happens it compromises collaboration, cooperation, and morale in ways that negatively impact productivity, performance, and results.

Team members may feel they were not treated fairly, not recognized for their contribution, or not supported when support was something they needed. When triggered by these social situations, the emotions involved may be frustration, anxiety, resentment, anger, or fear. Feeling heard and understood begins to shift and elevate the emotional state. When leaders ask questions in a sincere and caring way, it invites a feeling of safety in which an honest conversation can lead to resolution.

How can you use your constructive power to get to the heart of the matter of what took place so you can resolve the situation together?

_____

_____

_____

_____

_____

_____

_____

Think of a situation past or present in which team members were in a negative state. As a leader, how did you or could you address the negative state your team was experiencing? What conversations and what actions allowed you to elevate the negative state of your team to a positive one?

_____
_____
_____
_____
_____
_____
_____

Here's how NOT to elevate emotional states of mind and stay stuck in the reactive zone and negative team dynamics!

- Blame members of your team for everything that's going wrong. This way they'll know they're not in your good graces.

- Only listen to the perspectives of those you like or those who will agree with you. This sets up an excellent barrier to prevent honest communication and equitable outcomes from taking place.

- Be intimidating in a way that makes it difficult for team members to come to you with their concerns.

- Have your "busy-ness" take center stage in your priorities.

- Have your demeanor communicate your superiority and importance such as: "I have more important things to do than listen to you. Just get your job done. That's what you're being paid for."

- Hold people accountable in a judgmental way. Criticize them, point out their faults, hold them at arm's length, and withhold acknowledgement for anything they've done correctly. After all, this is what you expect them to do.

- Make people feel that expressing emotions is weak or just plain wrong!

The work you are doing to increase your relationship intelligence in terms of your team and their social needs helps you tap into the constructive power of *grace*. You can be a calm facilitator; listening generously, coming across as supportive rather than judgmental to reach satisfying resolutions when issues arise. This approach shortens the time lost to a negative emotional state. You can ask questions with authentic concern and curiosity to create the psychological safety needed for Trust. You can ask questions to open communication and elevate a negative emotional state that has compromised your team. You can neutralize negativity and restore an operating state that is positive and productive.

The BETA Model helps to define the direction to take in creating resolution and ensuring conditions for Belonging, Empowerment, Trust, and Alignment with your team. Each element of the BETA Model engages your constructive power to meet the needs of your team. In the present and the future, when you have integrated the constructive power available in the two pillars of *grace*, you will be able to bring out the best in people today and leave people better off for having known and worked with you in the future. As your relationship intelligence increases, you will become more adept at setting the conditions for high performance, high engagement, and high morale, even when the going gets tough. You will provide those you lead with the fulfillment of being a part of something meaningful together—something that is literally at the heart of the matter in being human and organizing our lives to make a difference.

Chapter 7

CHANGING A CULTURE WITH THE CONSTRUCTIVE POWER OF GRACE

The culture of an organization is the result of the way a leader leads. When a leader's efforts include the constructive power of *grace* and the knowledge of the social brain, the culture will benefit greatly. Many of the negative consequences that occur in a culture are the result of imbalances in *grit* and *gravitas* having been normalized.

A leader's approaches, behaviors, quality of their connection with people, and demeanor powerfully influence the social and psychological environment that distinguishes the culture of their organization. How a leader leads is the way people come to understand the rules of engagement and the values that are in play. In other words, it's a matter of what is acceptable and what is not. This is how behaviors become normalized in a culture.

Leadership: Critical choices and their impact in shaping a culture

When a leader takes the helm, there are many critical choices to be made. With leadership comes great responsibility and power. How will a leader use their power? Exemplary leaders use their power constructively. They intentionally create cultural conditions that meet the needs of their teams, their key peer relationships, and their stakeholders. They successfully build more collaborative, cross-functional relationships and create the conditions in which people feel safe to raise ideas, have difficult conversations, and solve challenges. As a result, silos and egos and win/lose survival patterns give way to cooperative norms that reinforced a sense of pride, allowing people to feel "we are all in this together." The most successful leaders intentionally set out to create a culture in which the conditions for achieving a sense of *Belonging, Empowerment, Trust,* and *Alignment* encourage and produce high morale and performance. The stage is set for people to be and do their best, feel a sense of appreciation and respect for each other, and take pride in the mission they are undertaking together.

Let's contrast this positive leadership approach toward a culture with one we describe as "political." In more political cultures, sustained negative emotional operating states often create costly negative consequences. The decrease in the conditions that meet the social brain's need for connection—for *Belonging, Empowerment, Trust,* and *Alignment*—creates win/lose survival patterns and triggers emotions such as anxiety, resentment, and fear, which exact a toll on productivity, engagement, and morale. Unlike the quality of attention and focus that occur when BETA conditions prevail in a culture, negative, adverse conditions compromise people's ability to focus on higher levels of innovative and objective thinking. The quality of people's attention becomes compromised by the concerns that people must deal with when they don't feel safe.

In these kinds of compromised conditions, what common triggers and reactions might employees find themselves dealing with? What have you noticed?

_____

_____

_____

_____

_____

_____

_____

_____

Healthy competitive cultures operate with integrity and have values-based rules of engagement. When employees take risks and put their all into an effort that could have a win or lose outcome, when they find difficulty in succeeding and they need to change course, they don't ignore the lesson—they learn. As a result, they increase their resilience and resolve; they regroup to become more effective.

In what ways could your leadership encourage and ensure the development of a healthy competitive culture? How could this help your team members become more effective?

_____

_____

_____

_____

_____

_____

_____

_____

Toxic cultures produce negative outcomes. The costs are profoundly personal in terms of the way people in the organization are impacted.

Leaders express their values and establish norms and patterns through their approaches, behaviors, quality of their connection with people, and demeanor. When a leader or group of leaders do not consciously attend to the quality of the culture, imbalances with *grit* and *gravitas* can disrupt the conditions that the social brain seeks for connection. When a leader lacks the constructive power of *grace*, they set the stage for toxic political dynamics to become normative in a culture.

Often the negative dynamics in a culture are the result of leaders who normalizes negative behaviors and obscure deception and unfair practices in play. Every leader has the opportunity to design the culture of their group, their organization, their division, and their team.

Consider the culture of your organization or other organizations you are familiar with. How does the presence or absence of *the constructive power of grace* along with imbalances in a leader's *grit* and *gravitas* contribute to political norms?

_____

_____

_____

_____

_____

_____

_____

_____

What norms, values, guidelines, and rules of engagement would best support the people you are leading?

_____

_____

_____

_____

_____

_____

How would this extend to the organization itself and the accomplishment of current strategy and goals?

_____

_____

_____

_____

_____

_____

What is missing that would inspire teamwork—collaboration, synergy, and alignment?

_____

_____

_____

_____

_____

_____

The constructive power of *grace* is not about being "nice." Nice can reflect an imbalance in which the social contract doesn't allow for healthy dialogue and pushing back in constructive ways that lead to sound decisions and breakthrough moments.

Imbalances in grit and gravitas are more common in the absence of BETA conditions.

A leader knowingly or unknowingly allowing a negative political culture to exist permits and empowers negative dynamics to dominate. Without the BETA conditions that fulfill the social needs of employees, the imbalances in *grit* and *gravitas* result in emotional operating states in which people may feel angry, anxious, frustrated, fearful, or resentful. The absence of BETA conditions then results in a decrease in morale and collaborative engagement. While some will try their best to work around the lack of collaboration and support, others will disengage in some form or another.

As you reflect on experiences you've had or observed, how does the absence of BETA conditions give rise to politics, and how do politics further contribute to the breakdown of the conditions for *Belonging, Empowerment, Trust,* and *Alignment*?

_____

_____

_____

_____

_____

_____

_____

_____

A leader's approaches, behaviors, and quality of how a leader interacts with the people they lead, as well as their demeanor can produce cultural dysfunction—negative politics where manipulations, deceptions, unfair practices result. Competitive behavior between interest groups that represent obstacles to cooperation, collaboration, and fair play will take their toll. They will obstruct efforts to come together to achieve common goals successfully.

The constructive power of *grace* is a benevolent force to lean in to, to improve, and elevate a culture. What steps change norms and behaviors? What steps can a leader take to ensure that BETA needs are able to be met?

_____

_____

_____

_____

_____

_____

_____

_____

_____

_____

_____

_____

_____

_____

Chapter 8

GRACE AND GENEROSITY

The social-emotional skills of *grace* are hallmarks of exemplary leadership. If you have experienced a leader's generosity, you have experienced moments when their capacity for *grace* was present. The exemplary leaders I have had the privilege of working with had a highly developed capacity of the constructive power of *grace*—as a result generosity was part of their character and was present in their approaches, their behaviors, in the quality of their connection with the people they led, and in their demeanor—their way of being.

One of the more distinctive qualities of *grace* in a leader's character is a generous approach toward people. Generosity is at the heart of the *constructive power of grace*. It is inseparable from the word *grace* because every time we choose our *constructive power,* every time we work to overcome our reactions, every time we restore our presence of mind and go beyond emotionally charged ways of responding to people, our generosity is involved. It takes generosity on the part of a leader to make the choice to lead with *constructive power.* Doing so is generous because it is much easier to lash out, criticize, withhold support when you don't like something someone did, or hold what they did against them. The absence of *grace* in a leader is the absence of a kind of compassionate generosity toward people—where a leader lacks the skills to get beyond reactions of blame, shame, and guilt to address problems and issues constructively. As a leader, it is generous to look more deeply, to get beyond an all-too-common reaction that you are right and someone else is wrong, to know your influence matters, and to be aware of the different outcomes that occur as a result of choosing constructive, positive approaches, rather than reactive, negative approaches.

What comes to mind when *you* consider the idea of generosity? Generosity takes many forms in a leader. For instance, people who are generous with their time, or generous in the way they take an interest in people, or generous in the way they listen, or pay attention to the needs of their employees, or in how they ensure a culture in which people can find meaningful engagement, and purpose.

What are some characteristics that describe leaders you've seen as generous; leaders who use their power in constructive ways?

_____

_____

_____

_____

_____

_____

_____

_____

In a social context generosity is a part of *relationship intelligence*. It involves skills and competences to move out of the reactive zone to facilitate interactions with others. For example, the interpersonal skills and to facilitate a discussion with members of your team to resolve differences and restore alignment. It is the quality of being kind and caring. Consider the difference in leaders who lack reaction management and re-lationship intelligence skills. If you unpack what is going on in the *reactive zone*, ego, power struggles, and right and wrong filtering that brings judgmental accusations to bear on others, you'll notice many opportunities to block mutual understanding and acceptance. Leaders who have developed their reaction management and relationship intelligence skills have a different level of mastery; the constructive power of *grace* balances and enhances their *grit* and their *gravitas*. The distinctions of the BETA Model are present in the cultures they create.

The absence of grace in a leader is the absence of a kind of generosity toward people. Generosity is the ability to get beyond and see beyond blame, shame, and guilt to address problems and issues constructively. It is generous to look more deeply, to get beyond an all-too-common reaction that you are right and someone else is wrong, to know your influence matters and to be aware of the different outcomes that occur because of choosing positive rather than negative approaches...

When a leader lacks generosity

A client recently demonstrated some of the imbalances that occur with *grit* and *gravitas* when the hallmark of exemplary leaders, a spirit of generosity, is missing in a leader's presence and impact. The client, talking about strengths she'd identified in herself, contrasted what she saw as her strengths with weaknesses she found in others. She spoke about attitudes she saw in other women in her organization in meetings with upper management. She said they sounded as if they lacked confidence or did not know what they were talking about. *"They lack gravitas,"* she said. The judgmental tone with which she described these other women revealed that she was not inclined to offer guidance to help them develop their *gravitas*. Even as she made insightful and important observations, she went no further than criticizing what she saw as their faults. She lacked the generosity to support and empower others to develop their potential.

GRACE AND GENEROSITY

What of value is lost when the spirit of generosity is not present in a leader? What could this client have accomplished in support of others, as well as what would have been of great benefit to the organization, had the *grit* and *gravitas* she possessed been infused with the *constructive power of grace*?

_____

_____

_____

_____

_____

_____

_____

_____

BILL AND ANIKA'S STORY

Sitting around a conference table, Bill, the COO of a large global organization, began to pointedly criticize Stephanie, a young manager who reported to the SVP Anika. As Bill's angry comments flew across the table, Stephanie, feeling conspicuously criticized in front of everyone at the table, began to shrink back in shame and embarrassment. Anika leaned forward, her posture almost shielding Stephanie, and calmly addressed Bill by outlining the background information and the logic and reason for what Stephanie had shared. Anika's approach created an immediate shift in the tension in the room, which served to neutralize the negativity coming across the table and allowed a productive conversation to follow. The tenor of the conversation shifted away from criticism and blame as Anika skillfully intervened, creating the conditions for the issues at hand to be constructively resolved.

Following the meeting, Stephanie let Anika know how much she appreciated her support. Other attendees let Anika know they'd never seen anything like that with

93

questions and statements such as "How did you do that?" and "That was amazing!" Generously, she gave Bill the benefit of the doubt, knowing he was mainly a very fair and even-tempered person and that he must for some reason be having a bad day. She had the presence of mind to take a constructive approach and avoided calling him out in front of everyone when she intervened on Stephanie's behalf. She acted in a way that created psychological safety for Stephanie and everyone else at the table.

What skills are involved in being able to diffuse a reactive situation in the way that Anika did?

_____

_____

_____

_____

_____

_____

_____

What is the value of using one's generosity in being able to look beyond reactions to a negative situation and to forego opinions that would be easy to form about someone?

_____

_____

_____

_____

_____

_____

_____

Let's take a moment to consider what occurred in terms of how Anika integrated the *constructive power of grace* and how it flowed generously through her approaches, her behaviors, the quality of her connection with those involved, and her demeanor.

What can you see in the **approaches** she took?

_____
_____
_____
_____
_____
_____
_____
_____
_____

What can you see in her **behaviors**?

_____
_____
_____
_____
_____
_____
_____
_____
_____

What was the quality of her **connection** with the people involved?

_____

_____

_____

_____

_____

_____

_____

_____

What was evident in her **demeanor**?

_____

_____

_____

_____

_____

_____

_____

_____

_____

Anika used the _constructive power of grace_ to alter the direction of a sudden reactive situation for the better. Our next example is about a leader who used the _constructive power of grace_ to confront a reactive situation that was brought to her attention, one in which anger and animosity between two employees had been festering for a long time.

Michele's story is an example of how a leader's willingness and generosity resolved a seemingly impossible situation.

Michele was the COO of a group of medical offices. She highly valued the physicians and staff who worked in each of the offices she oversaw. Each office was run by a physician leader, and although the culture of each office differed as a result, every employee shared an understanding of what was expected of them in terms of their individual performance as well as the overall performance of each office. Michele's commitment and dedication as a leader were evident in the constructive approaches she took, the respect and transparency of her behaviors, and the caring, empowering ways she connected with people, as well as the calm objectivity that came across in her demeanor.

As in many organizations, there are times when staff members don't get along, when tempers flare, when there are instances of people not pulling their weight. And there are also times when more serious situations arise. Michele's direct reports took care of many of these problems. Still, they also knew they could count on her to provide wise counsel when they brought more difficult situations to her attention.

One of her direct reports came to her with an escalating situation occurring between two doctors that had reached a crisis point. Michele asked for help in facilitating a resolution. The process started by meeting with each doctor individually. To establish trust and psychological safety, Michele assured each of them that they had her full support and commitment. She told them she would assist them in finding a way to resolve their differences—acknowledging that this might not seem possible to them at the moment. In these preliminary, confidential sessions, they each shared their perspective of why circumstances were the way they were and the reasons they found themselves in this highly charged, unworkable situation with one another.

Dr. Robinson was the physician leader of this particular office, responsible for over-seeing the quality of patient care. He was someone with a great deal of intelligence, expertise, and commitment to the quality of their work with patients. He had a desire for his staff to feel they were a part of something meaningful where each of their roles mattered. Yet here he was, dealing with the lack of cooperation and alignment from a member of his team—Dr. Miller—which had become an insurmountable obstacle. He knew something needed to be done to face and deal with the situation.

One of the main problems Dr. Robinson described was a lack of respect he felt from Dr. Miller regarding his responsibilities ensuring the quality of patient care. In far too many interactions with Dr. Miller, he'd not only felt a lack of respect from her; he found her to be uncooperative, resistant, and inconsiderate. Dr. Robinson shared that he'd never had this kind of situation before, and it had become intolerable for him to work with her. He was very concerned about the staff in the office he oversaw. The staff members had taken sides and split into two camps, which made the workplace much more difficult. His attempts to talk with Dr. Miller and to reason with her had led nowhere, and he now knew without a doubt that working with her was no longer possible.

Dr. Miller shared that she felt threatened by the actions Dr. Robinson took to ensure the quality of service that had to do with her work. She saw his actions as a lack of respect for her work. She felt that she had worked hard to establish herself and build her patient practice. She resisted what she saw as his attempts "to control" her.

Work in an organization is a social phenomenon, a place where there are social con-tracts around the interfacing of roles and responsibilities. People are accountable to the person they report to; in this case, Dr. Miller reported to Dr. Robinson. The social contract was that he was to oversee the quality of all work performed in that office—including hers.

Dr. Miller shared that she didn't understand why he needed to go over her cases with her when she was "a good physician" who knew what she was doing. She resented him asking about her work. Dr. Miller had taken great offense the prior week when, as she was finishing up a procedure with a client, he'd come into the room to see how things had gone. Afterwards she was so enraged at him for having done this. The annoyance and animosity she felt toward him escalated into another heated argument.

Part of psychological safety is having the chance to express thoughts and feelings that are difficult to say. The next part of the process was organized for the purpose of facilitating a resolution through direct communication between Dr. Miller and Dr. Robinson. Sitting around the table together, Michele reminded them of the importance of taking this opportunity to communicate openly with one another. She stressed the importance of finding a resolution, noting that this situation was costly to each of them personally as well as to the organization. She told them she was counting on them to have an honest discussion about what led up to this situation in the hopes that a resolution to the problem could be found. If not, she would find herself in a situation in which she would feel forced to make a decision she would rather not have to make.

Why is resolution difficult in this type of process?

_____

_____

_____

_____

_____

_____

_____

_____

Without understanding and compassion when reactions reach an impasse, a resolution can seem unachievable. Is there a time you've experienced something like this?

_____

_____

_____

_____

_____

_____

_____

In the *reactive zone*, the sense of connection between people is temporarily disabled. Accusations and defensiveness about who is right and who is wrong get in the way of seeing someone as a human being rather than as "the enemy" and get in the way of seeing through the lens of understanding and compassion. It is important to be able to understand another's struggle, another's vulnerability, another's pain.

Both Dr. Robinson and Dr. Miller felt threatened. Their reactions flew across the table at the enemy they saw sitting across from them—each other. Then came the moment in the process when it looked as though a resolution would be impossible to achieve. Dr. Robinson got up from the table and walked out of the room saying, "I can't see this working out, and I don't want to work with you any longer." His words were blunt and direct. Door closed. Game over.

Dr. Robinson's words hung in the air with finality. Stunned, Dr. Miller realized that her worst fears might have just been confirmed. She struggled to find her footing as worried thoughts and emotions swirled around in her mind, the difficulties she would have to face of relocating, of rebuilding her practice, of having to change her daughter's school, and of losing the friends she'd made.

Without the presence of understanding and compassion, when reactions reach this kind of impasse, a resolution can seem unachievable. Would it surprise you to know that the relationship between them improved and resolved from there? It takes a willingness and a generosity on one's part to find a way, especially because compassion, while part of what it is to be human, can become blunted by anger and misunderstanding. When we begin to understand each other, our compassion can emerge without effort.

Have you experienced a time when, in a difficult situation, understanding and compassion changed the situation for the better?

_____

_____

_____

_____

_____

_____

_____

_____

Dr. Robinson asked to speak to us privately. Michele, committed to facilitating the resolution, joined the conversation. She shared a personal story of her own about how she once found herself in a stressful, competitive situation with a colleague. She decided to have a conversation with this colleague. She addressed their competitive dynamics and suggested that if they worked together, instead of against each other, they could form an alliance that would make them exceedingly successful as a team. Her colleague took her up on her suggestion and everything changed—for the better. From that moment on their relationship became a "powerhouse that distinguished them both."

After sharing this story with Dr. Robinson, Michele said, "I understand if you don't want to continue. I will respect your decision either way but, as a leader, isn't it valuable to be able to deal effectively with people who are being difficult?"

How was this situation an opportunity for Dr. Robinson to develop as a leader?

_____

_____

_____

_____

_____

_____

_____

_____

Michele asked Dr. Robinson to find a way to transcend all the acrimony in the situation to heal his relationship with Dr. Miller and resolve the rift that had affected everyone in the office. She asked him to consider what might be underneath Dr. Miller's reactions and behaviors. Would he be surprised to learn that although he saw her as competent, she did not realize that? She thought he was questioning her work because he didn't think she was doing a good job.

We then shared some of the other comments Dr. Miller had taken the risk of expressing when Dr. Robinson had angrily left the room. He became aware of challenges Dr. Miller was dealing with as a single parent and how hard it had been for her to establish her roots there. He began to understand what it must feel like for her and how hard it would be, given his refusal to work with her any longer, for her to have to leave and start all over again.

In that moment, Dr. Robinson saw Dr. Miller as a human being with personal vulnerabilities, challenges, and professional aspirations she'd worked hard to achieve. Through this lens he was able to understand her fears and concerns. His compassion emerged as he began to understand how she had been struggling. Dr. Robinson decided to take the opportunity Michele had suggested—to evolve as a leader. He found himself saying, "I want to hit the reset button and go on in a better way."

Dr. Robinson returned to the conference room where Dr. Miller was waiting. As the two made eye contact, immediately she could see and feel the shift in his expression and his demeanor; the anger was gone. He put out his hand to Dr. Miller and said, "Let's hit the reset button and go on in a better way together. I really respect you. I think you are an extremely competent physician. You've come such a long way. My responsibility for quality and operations in our office in no way is meant to make you feel that I don't value and respect you. I'm not trying to check up on you because I don't think you are competent, but I can see that it could feel that way to you. You are extremely competent. I'm just trying to do what I've been asked to do."

In addition, he said, "What if we thought about a goal we could have where we collaborate regarding the quality of service to our clients? We could get together on a regular basis and identify our most effective approaches and outcomes. We could generate a compendium of our best practices and even share them with others in our group. How does this sound to you?"

She expressed her appreciation for the opportunity to go on in a better way. She was surprised and relieved, not having expected the situation to work out. She felt a genuine sense of connection and alignment and was grateful for a positive way to go forward together. Dr. Miller also expressed the respect she had for Dr. Robinson's experience and expertise. She let him know she valued his knowledge and felt she could learn a great deal from him.

In this example, the drama of the situation had escalated to an unworkable point. Yet, after several difficult conversations, moments of grace, compassion, and understanding had emerged. No one was more surprised than they were. Part of the spirit of generosity involves the desire to reawaken our compassion when it shuts down.

Healing the divide…

The office staff were used to seeing Dr. Robinson and Dr. Miller at odds with one another. As a critical part of hitting the reset button, they gathered their staff together the next day. Together both doctors shared that they had resolved their differences and acknowledged how difficult things had been. The staff was relieved and felt reassured that the animosity between them had been resolved. Together they worked on how they would all go forward in a better way. Dr. Robinson and Dr. Miller led the way to establishing and sustaining a reset of their culture.

Michele could have taken a very different approach in handling this critical situation. Given her commitment to the people she leads and her dedication to ensuring that employees are empowered in their mission to provide the highest level of care, she chose to invest her time and resources and have professional guidance to generate a breakthrough if possible. She knew she was taking a risk, but she saw the potential upside as significant. If it worked out, she would be able to salvage the fine talent she already had in place, elevate their emotional state from a negative to a positive one, and help them find a way to restore a sense of Belonging, Empowerment, Trust, and Alignment—all of which represented a win for everyone.

Let's review what occurred in terms of how Dr. Robinson and Dr. Miller finally found the compassion and understanding they needed to be able to integrate the *constructive power of grace* into their *grit* and *gravitas*.

What shifted in their approaches toward one another?

_____

_____

_____

_____

_____

_____

_____

What shifted in their behavior?

_____

_____

_____

_____

_____

_____

_____

What shifted in the quality of their connection with one another?

_____

_____

_____

_____

_____

_____

_____

What shifted in their demeanor toward each other and their organization?

_____

_____

_____

_____

_____

_____

_____

_____

Let's consider generosity:

Was it generous on Dr. Robinson's part to reconsider his reactions to what he saw as Dr. Miller's lack of cooperation? What became possible as a result?

_____

_____

_____

_____

_____

_____

_____

_____

Was it generous to take some responsibility and to choose to evolve as a leader, rather than walk away from the situation? What do you see about this?

_____
_____
_____
_____
_____
_____
_____
_____

Why does generosity matter? What does it make possible that is of value to all?

_____
_____
_____
_____
_____
_____
_____
_____

When you care enough to be willing to resolve a conflict, your willingness to understand another's experience is generous. It helps you awaken your compassion. Compassion changes your emotional state toward someone, replacing the lack of awareness and hardheadedness that come from the imbalances of *grit* and *gravitas* with the mindful openheartedness of *grace*.

What difference can you see this having in the dynamics between people on teams and on the culture of an organization?

_____

_____

_____

_____

_____

_____

_____

There is always the choice to be made as to how to deal with challenges that arise. Every time we turn to the *constructive power of grace* to address difficulties, break-downs, and challenges, the spirit of generosity is active. It brings about important outcomes and benefits such as the way leaders can elevate people's emotional state from negative to positive and to increase participation and engagement. Generosity is at the heart of the *constructive power of grace*. It is inseparable from the word *grace* because every time you choose constructive power over reactive, emotionally charged ways of responding to people, your generosity will be making an important difference.

It takes generosity for people to get past these kinds of reactive situations—generosity for oneself and for the other people involved in the reaction. It takes commitment to be aware in the moment of a reaction and to discipline yourself to mentally pause and step outside of it. When a reaction takes over, it can be difficult to "break the spell." It isn't always easy to find the pause button. Some reactions are easier than others to "shake off." But until you break "the spell" of a reaction, your stress response will extract a physical and emotional toll. In the midst of reactions, people—yourself and others—feel emotional pain. Who wouldn't welcome a lifeline of compassion and understanding, an olive branch of forgiveness, or jump at the chance to go on in a better way?

Chapter 9

USING GRIT, GRACE, AND GRAVITAS TO PREVAIL IN ADVERSITY

Many of our clients have found themselves challenged by power struggles and inequities due to working in an adverse, political environment where destructive behavior is tolerated. More than a few of the situations these clients faced involved a boss, direct report, or colleague whose goal was to undermine others. They draw attention to themselves to elevate their self-importance at the *expense* of others. Their negative approaches and behaviors, the intimidating ways they connect with people, and the arrogance present in their demeanor ensured they were the dominant power player in their organization. Let's consider this, along with Dr. Gavin Dagley's research, in which respondents defined a *negative* or *dark presence* as follows:

Negative interpersonal behavior patterns and values-in-action included: "behaviors in four areas: **aggression** (that such people were 'critical,' 'intimidating,' 'judgmental,' 'condescending,' 'demeaning,' 'bullying,' 'hostile,' and 'overbearing'); **aloofness** (the person's behaviors were 'cold,' 'dismissive,' and 'remote'); **political behavior** (the person was 'manipulative,' and good at 'managing upwards'); and finally,

unpredictability (including '[you] never knew where you stood,' a lack of openness, and the person 'kept everyone on edge'). Values-in-action responses included comments about arrogance, dishonesty, intolerance, the primacy of personal agendas, and distrustfulness of others" (Dagley, 2013, p. 10).

IRENE'S STORY

Irene is a remarkably dedicated and accomplished professional in a financial services firm. Year after year she succeeded in surpassing the results of the previous year. We will look at how she was able to accomplish this while having to contend with a colleague, Brad, who sought to undermine her efforts.

Irene and Brad were peers who were on equal footing as partners in their last company before merging with another financial services firm. Although Brad and Irene both had partner status in the new entity, Irene noticed that Brad was aggressively seeking advancement. When larger client opportunities came about, he made sure they were given to him. Concurrently, the incidences of Brad treating Irene with disrespect increased, as did occurrences of discrediting her behind her back.

Irene was informed by her current boss that the company was reorganizing, and she would now be reporting to Brad. She asked if there was a way to continue to report to her current boss but was told that with the reorganization that wouldn't be possible. Irene had a great deal of concern and trepidation as the transition took place. In terms of who she was to report to and was told there was no other option.

Irene knew, without a doubt, that this change was not in her best interest. Her concerns were confirmed almost immediately. Brad's negative attitude toward her became increasingly problematic. He continued to withhold client opportunities from her. He wrested accounts out from under her that she had secured for the firm, and he found ways of taking credit for results she'd been instrumental in delivering.

Brad's negativity toward Irene came to her attention in other ways. Colleagues let her know of demeaning remarks made behind her back. Whenever Irene presented to their group, Brad's disinterest in what she was presenting would be expressed by his working on his phone or by his leaving the room and not returning. Whatever his motivation—ego? control issues? competitive power plays?—his behavior toward her stemmed from some need on his part to diminish her directly, as well as in the eyes of others, and to prevent her from gaining status and recognition. Brad's actions are examples of a leader's negative or dark presence.

Gossip aimed at having someone be less well thought of is a damaging ploy with lasting effects. Irene spent most of her time on the road serving clients, but there were also times she worked from the home office. Because Brad had gossiped about her and discredited her behind her back, Irene felt ill at ease working in their home office when Brad was there.

Before we look at how Irene handled this challenging situation with Brad, you are probably wondering why she didn't just leave the firm. Here are some of the reasons. Irene cared about the client relationships she had built up over the years, people who she was dedicated to, people who valued her support and guidance. She didn't want to lose them. She had earned the trust and respect of these clients, which meant a great deal to Irene. She also didn't want to lose newer clients she was in the midst of advising. There was also a very restrictive non-compete agreement to take into consideration. After decades of hard work, she did not relish the idea of what she would have to forego to start all over again.

On several occasions, Irene tried to have a conversation with Brad to neutralize the negativity she felt and improve their dynamics. Her efforts were unsuccessful. Communication to resolve unworkable dynamics can produce miracles, but that only happens when all parties involved share a sincere commitment to resolve issues. Irene realized that working things out with Brad was not something she could achieve. How could Irene mitigate the negative impact of Brad's disrespectful and judgmental

111

behavior, including the damage he'd done gossiping about her behind the scenes? In our conversations she shared that this negativity had affected her self-confidence. She decided to concentrate her efforts in a different direction, one that would help her lift her emotional state to a more positive one and help build her confidence from within.

Irene focused on increasing her well-being, as well as strengthening her core sense of respect and regard for the consummate professional she is. She became more and more present to the value she added and her contributions to the growth of the firm. Irene set personal boundaries, shifting her habit of needing validation from Brad and not allowing the inequities she'd been up against to harden her heart. She put together a chronology of the negative actions and injustices that had occurred, updating it as any further situations took place. Having this record at her disposal served as an important resource. It shifted her perspective from feeling victimized by the situation to feeling confident that she could handle this in a powerful way at the right time. She would be ready to stand up for herself when the opportunity presented itself.

The objective viewpoint she secured for herself gave her the distance she needed from taking Brad's behavior personally. She was able to see Brad as someone operating with a very different set of values and ethics. At that time she needed to do some work to build her confidence in her considerable knowledge and experience.

Irene worked on clarifying her internal bearings. She identified what she held most dear in being a trusted advisor, which included her aspirations for making a difference in meeting her clients' needs and contributing at a high level to her organization's success.

Irene came to recognize and appreciate that the *constructive power of grace* was a superpower that came naturally to her. The *grace* that flowed through her *grit* and her *gravitas* was observable in her approaches, her behaviors, the quality of how she connected with people, and her demeanor.

How did Dagley's definition of *dark presence* play a role in this situation?

_____

_____

_____

_____

_____

_____

How do you set boundaries, protect yourself, and apply what the *constructive power of grace* can offer you in these kinds of situations?

_____

_____

_____

_____

_____

_____

_____

What was in Irene's control, and what wasn't?

_____

_____

_____

_____

_____

_____

_____

Chapter 10

CONCLUSION: GRACE IS THE GAME CHANGER

We have seen time and again that what distinguishes exemplary leaders is their capacity for *grace*. Their *grit* and their *gravitas*, infused with the skills and qualities of *grace*, bring exceptional value to those they lead. Great leaders understand and embrace the responsibilities that go beyond their job descriptions. They welcome the opportunities to inspire and bring out the best in those they lead. They set out to generate a culture in which people thrive, have a sense of being a part of something meaningful, and feel empowered, valued, and appreciated.

Take a few moments to reflect about which qualities and skills of the constructive power of *grace* you can put into practice right away, to elevate your own *grit* and *gravitas*? Make some initial notes you can return to and develop further:

_____

_____

_____

_____

_____

_____

Exemplary leaders have worked to develop their *reaction management* and *relationship intelligence* skills. They have earned the trust, respect, and affection of those they lead because they understand, pay attention to, and listen well to people, they treat people with respect and compassion. Exemplary leaders develop teams of people who are in step with one another to accomplish the outcomes that matter. Together they face the challenges that come with the hard times and share pride in the successes that are part of the good times.

Today more and more leaders are increasing their self-awareness. They are choosing to address imbalances in their *grit* and *gravitas* and achieve the transformations their *constructive power* makes possible. Taking steps to define and develop their *highest leadership aspirations* is providing them with a sustained sense of purpose with which to shape their impact. These leaders are honing their ability to *elevate emotional operating states* and inspire those they lead through the tough times. As one client put it, they like themselves *"better this way."*

Presence, it turns out, is no mystery. It isn't a function of having charisma or a larger-than-life personality. It doesn't require you to be an extrovert. It is important to remember that you are the one who decides the quality, substance, and impact of your presence. It is totally in your hands to decide which qualities and skills will help you evolve your leadership, your presence, and your impact. A place to begin is to pay attention to the effect your presence is currently having on those you lead. Secondly, you can ask for feedback and objectively look at the imbalances that are brought to your attention. For instance, as one leader shared, *"I need to increase my reaction management and learn to pause and choose a constructive way to respond to situations that are hard for me to handle."*

Which qualities and skills will help you to evolve as a leader? Be honest with yourself. Start with one or two changes you want to make. Big changes are the result of small steps taken, one after the other.

_____

_____

_____

_____

_____

_____

_____

_____

A leader's evolution doesn't happen all at once. In a quiet moment you may realize that you have a greater sense of well-being; you may notice positive feedback coming from your colleagues, family, and those you lead. You may notice differences in how you are relating to others, how you are handling upsets, and how your efforts are having a constructive impact on people, productivity, and results.

In the process of your development, each of the efforts you make is important to the growth you are working to achieve. As you take risks and practice using the *constructive power of grace,* remember that the changes you make—no matter how small they may seem to you—will produce a momentum, a cumulative positive effect that will be beneficial for you and those you lead. Reminding ourselves of the guiding skills and qualities of *grace,* we can bring out the best in people through our considerate, thoughtful, and stabilizing efforts, even in the worst of circumstances.

The more you succeed in infusing your grit and gravitas with the skills and qualities of grace you will come to realize how much this matters. You will see first-hand, how turning to and relying on your constructive power changes your leadership, changes your presence, changes the impact you are able to have—for the better. You will become aware of how the efforts you are making are bringing about benevolent changes in your life and in the lives of the people you lead.

We are living and working in very challenging times. But we are also, as Arianna Huffington reminds us in her book *The Fourth Instinct*, "facing a door in time… an opening for great possibilities of a new being, for a breakthrough in our evolution." "For the first time," she tells us, "something as vast and epic as the destiny of mankind depends on something as personal and intimate as the way each one of us chooses to live, think, and behave." Our capacity to be constructive in our approaches, in our behaviors, in the quality of how we connect with one another, and in our demeanors is greatly needed. Critical breakthroughs depend on the social-emotional skills that bring us together to collaborate, solve, and innovate—in science, technology, medicine, governance, education, commerce, finance, conservation, and in the disciplines of every organization, in every walk of life.

With our grit, grace, and gravitas, may each of us reach inward to harness our potential to evolve, reach outward to support and empower those we live and work with, and reach across to connect in meaningful ways that generate human understanding and breakthroughs. With the constructive power of grace may we not only transcend the divides that have existed until now, may we stand on our common ground with dignity and elevate the future for us all. We can do this.

ABOUT THE AUTHORS

Jane Firth advises executives and their teams and is an innovator in the areas of leadership performance and executive presence. Jane is the originator and author of *Grit, Grace, & Gravitas: The Three Keys to Transforming Leadership, Presence, and Impact*. Her work facilitates the advancement, stature, contribution, and recognition of leaders and executives. For her outstanding work, Jane was awarded the Philadelphia Business Journal's Women of Distinction Award. She has an MSOD from the University of Pennsylvania, is a founder of the University of Pennsylvania Center for Organizational Dynamics, and is a founder of the Psychoanalytic Coaches Association. Jane is a long-standing member of the Forum of Executive Women and has chaired the Women in Executive Leadership and Governance Committee. In addition, Jane is a co-founding partner of Globalislocal and the Beyond our Differences Foundation. She's served on the Board of Advisors of NDRI, the board of the Pyramid Club, and the board of Women's Philanthropy. For more information go to firthleadershippartners.com.

Andrea Zintz, Ph.D., is president of Strategic Leadership Resources and has over 40 years' experience in organization development, leadership development, and coaching. Before starting her own consulting practice, she served in two executive roles at Johnson & Johnson: as Vice President of Human Resources for the J&J subsidiary Ortho Biotech, Inc., and as Director Leadership Development at J&J Corporate Headquarters. Andrea received her B.S. in business communications from Emerson College and her M.A. and Ph.D. from Fielding Graduate University. Andrea is a recipient of the YWCA Tribute to Women in Industry Award. She currently is a member of the National Organizational Development (OD) Network and has co-authored the book *Orchestrating Sustainable Innovation: A Symphony in Sound Bites* (available at Amazon). For more information go to strategicleadershipresources.com.